Praise for *The Adam Quest*

"To a debate that usually provokes accusations, name-calling, and polarization, Tim Stafford offers a wise, mediating overview. For some, this book may well be a faith-saver."

—PHILIP YANCEY, AUTHOR OF *WHAT GOOD IS GOD?*

"If you've ever been troubled by the relationship between science, the Bible, and human origins—this book is for you. Tim is thoughtful of mind and generous of spirit—two qualities much needed in this discussion."

—JOHN ORTBERG, SENIOR PASTOR OF MENLO PARK PRESBYTERIAN CHURCH, AND AUTHOR OF *WHO IS THIS MAN?*

"Tim Stafford provides a glimpse into the lives of eleven scientists with a strong commitment to Christian faith who are involved in the creation/evolution controversies, representing different perspectives. He goes beyond the technical details of the debates to reveal the personal experiences that underlie each of their convictions. Everyone interested in science and faith would benefit from this insightful perspective of the human sentiment behind the wide range of positions."

—RANDY ISAAC, EXECUTIVE DIRECTOR, AMERICAN SCIENTIFIC AFFILIATION

"The importance of Stafford's book is that it brings together the top advocates of the various creation positions and lets them speak for themselves. The personal stories put a human face on a debate that has split Christians from Christians, as well as Christians from non-Christians. I found the discussion of the personal histories of each author as important as the technical positions they defend. This is as much a book about the sociology of science as the details of creation. It lays out how science advances, how Christians practice their faith in their discipline, and how the science establishment responds to propositions that are not in the mainstream."

—ROBERT K. PRUD'HOMME, PROFESSOR OF CHEMICAL AND BIOLOGICAL ENGINEERING; DIRECTOR, PROGRAM IN ENGINEERING BIOLOGY AT PRINCETON UNIVERSITY

"The words 'science' and 'religion' placed side by side more often than not result in spontaneous combustion. Fiery invective and contention blaze from both sides. Tim Stafford brings a breath of fresh air in the stench of invective that has characterized language used between science and religion since the days of Galileo. He uses words between old rivals conversationally, listening words of mutual respect."

—EUGENE H. PETERSON, PROFESSOR EMERITUS OF SPIRITUAL THEOLOGY, REGENT COLLEGE, VANCOUVER, B.C.

"Tim Stafford's book is unique and impressive in the breadth of viewpoints presented by thoughtful Christian scholars. They clearly have profound differences in their approach to biblical exegesis and interpretation of scientific knowledge. At the same time, each expresses an abiding faith in Christ and an unmistakable love of science. What these scientists share is far greater than the controversies that separate them. Stafford wants all of us to appreciate this as well, and his book is a big step toward fulfilling his hope."

—ROBERT KAITA, PHYSICIST AT PRINCETON UNIVERSITY

"In *The Adam Quest* Tim set out to improve the tone of the debate about human origins. In my mind he succeeded. By promising to serve as a reporter rather than a polemicist, he gained the trust of advocates across the spectrum of positions on the subject. As a result we encounter eleven very different scientists as persons instead of protagonists. The result is a new window into the debate—or better yet, some oil on troubled waters."

—JACK C. SWEARENGEN, PhD, PROFESSOR OF ENGINEERING (RETIRED); AUTHOR OF *BEYOND PARADISE? TECHNOLOGY AND THE KINGDOM OF GOD* the adam quest

the adam quest

eleven scientists who held on to
a strong faith while wrestling with
the mystery of human origins

Tim Stafford

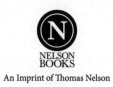

NELSON
BOOKS

An Imprint of Thomas Nelson

Published in Nashville, Tennessee, by Nelson Books, an imprint of Thomas Nelson. Nelson Books and Thomas Nelson are registered trademarks of HarperCollins Christian Publishing, Inc.

Thomas Nelson, Inc., titles may be purchased in bulk for educational, business, fund-raising, or sales promotional use. For information, please e-mail SpecialMarkets@ ThomasNelson.com.

Scripture quotations are taken from the Holy Bible, New International Version®, NIV®. Copyright © 1973, 1978, 1984 by Biblica, Inc.™ Used by permission of Zondervan. All rights reserved worldwide. www.zondervan.com.

ISBN: 978-0-5291-0271-3 (IE)

Library of Congress Cataloging-in-Publication Data

Stafford, Tim, 1950-
 The Adam quest : eleven scientists explore the divine mystery of human origins / Tim Stafford.
    pages cm
 Includes bibliographical references and index.
 ISBN 978-1-4002-0564-6
1. Religion and science. 2. Scientists--Religious life. 3. Scientists--Biography--20th century. 4. Human beings--Origin. I. Title.
 BL240.3.S723 2013
 215'.7--dc23

                                    2013012261

Printed in the United States of America

13 14 15 16 17 RRD 6 5 4 3 2 1

Contents

1 Introduction

I have a son who has struggled to find peace with God. I don't completely understand the nature of this struggle, but from the time Silas was a teenager I knew that it tormented him. I found this a very hard struggle to watch. As a believing parent, you want more than anything else for your children to build a solid foundation of faith. You can't do it for them. All you can do is encourage them and pray for them and try to open up the right kinds of opportunities for them to grow.

Silas went to church and youth group, but I don't think he ever really made deep spiritual friendships there. That was why, toward the end of Silas's high school years, my wife and I encouraged him to apply for work at a nearby Christian camp. We hoped that he would make friends with serious Christians of his own age, people who were fun and smart and able to talk about deep questions.

Silas worked at that camp for two summers. He did, as we had hoped, make good friends. I can't say that he stopped struggling with faith, but he seemed to move in good directions.

The friends stayed in touch even after they all went off to college. But then something went wrong. Silas got burned by the fight over Genesis.

During his senior year in high school, Silas had taken a class in geology at our local junior college. The professor was an excellent teacher with a passion for his subject. Silas caught the vision, and he decided to major in geology.

Geology field trips in his freshman year of college took Silas into the mountains and deserts of California. In short order he mastered the basics of reading the history of the rocks. But then he began to experience conflict with his camp friends. They insisted that the earth was young, according to the Bible. If Silas wanted to be a serious Christian, he had to get out of geology. Whatever geologists believed about the age of the earth was completely wrong.

I doubt this would have bothered Silas too deeply if the friends had just offered their point of view and then agreed to disagree. They were insistent, however. They could not let the subject alone. I imagine that they felt they were courageous Christians, speaking up for scriptural truth and refusing to let a friend go down the path of ungodliness. In practice, though, they drove Silas away from faith. He needed fellowship, but he couldn't handle their attitude.

For geologists, the earth is obviously billions of years old. Asking them to think differently is like asking your astronomer friend to believe that the sun circles around the earth. From Silas's perspective, his friends just didn't know what they were talking about. If you want to believe in nonsense, be my guest, but please don't righteously insist that everybody else believe the same nonsense.

There were probably other factors in their rift, but the clash between science and the Bible was certainly a big part of the struggle. Silas fell out with the whole circle. (Years later, at a camp reunion, they had a warm encounter. But by then the damage was done. They weren't going to pick up the friendship where they had left off years before.)

This was the first time I experienced firsthand the damage that can be done when science and faith are at odds. It hurt my son in an area of deep importance, and I felt it.

I grew up in a devout Bible-believing Christian home, where questions about human origins were only occasionally discussed. My parents were open to the possibility that Noah's flood was local, not universal, and that the six days of creation might refer to long periods of time. But they believed the creator God—not random and directionless processes—was at the center of the story. They sensed that evolution could eliminate God from that story, a possibility they would never accept.

They were not dogmatic about details of God's creation. I have the distinct impression that it did not seem all that critical to them to settle all questions about the history of the earth. They thought of it as a matter of secondary importance, like modes of baptism.

I inherited those attitudes. As far back as I can remember, questions of creation were interesting to me, and I was willing to contemplate a variety of points of view. I instinctively felt doubts about evolution, and when I read a critique like Phillip Johnson's *Darwin on Trial*, a seminal text in the Intelligent Design movement, I found it interesting and significant. However, I didn't become a true believer. I didn't think too much was at stake.

When Silas crashed into these questions, though, it suddenly became a big deal to me. I began to pay closer attention not only to the issues as I understood them but also to people in science and the frustrations they feel.

For years I'd held an on-and-off discussion with Bob Messing, a friend who heads a microbiology research lab associated with the University of California, San Francisco. Now I listened to Bob more carefully. I grasped how frustrated he was with his church—a solid, biblical church—and I saw how that frustration was slowly eroding Bob's faith. Bob loved that church community, who had supported him through hard times, but he felt he could not relate to their views about science. "Everything I do is based on evolution," he told me. But evolution was a conversation stopper within the walls of his church. Members there viewed evolution with uninformed skepticism, if not hostility.

Bob tried hard to change that. He volunteered to lead an adult class that looked at Christian critiques of evolution. In that class Bob tried to explain why none of those critiques had any traction in the scientific community. He felt people listened but didn't really hear.

Biological research was the single most important reality in Bob's life. He loved his church community, but he lived his research. His work, Bob felt, would never be fully embraced in his church.

I realize Bob's situation is complicated. Reactions to God and to the community of believers always mix reality and rationalization. Unquestionably, though, that church's skepticism about science played an important role in Bob's drifting away.

It's so for many scientists I've talked to. Others hold them at a distance because of their work. It often stops conversations cold. When it doesn't, people who don't know enough science to properly understand the issues may nevertheless lecture them about evolution. If the scientists are committed believers, it's a constant irritant. If they start out on the far edges of faith, these attitudes will keep them there.

––––––––––

There's a flip side, of course. Scientists can be arrogant know-it-alls. Some of the premier scientific spokespersons today make a point of baiting Christians, proclaiming that science has disproved religious belief. When they tell the story of how life evolved, they speak as though it's a scientific fact that the whole process is pointless and godless.

While Silas and Bob lost faith because of Christians' attitudes toward science, lots of other people have lost faith because they listened to scientists.

For much of the nineteenth century, what's called *scientific positivism* insisted that truth had to be testable and repeatable. If you couldn't run a scientific experiment on it, it wasn't worth talking about. This frame of mind came to dominate much thinking. The famous New Testament scholar Rudolf Bultmann wrote, "It is impossible to use electric light . . . and to avail ourselves of modern medical and surgical discoveries, and at the same time to believe in the New Testament world of spirits and miracles."[1] Bultmann didn't intend to undermine faith, but he did. Lots of people jumped to the conclusion that the Bible was full of unbelievable fiction from a bygone era. Once they stopped trusting Scripture, they drifted away from godly attitudes and beliefs. They embraced moral relativism and came to doubt that truth was anything more than someone's opinion. No wonder many Christians became skittish about science.

For some time, we've been in a state of cold war between science and faith, especially in America. Discussions about how evolution should be taught in school sometimes end up as court cases. When they do, the cold war flares into an apocalyptic battle. Christians who don't believe in evolution think it's unfair that evolution is the only position that is presented. Scientists and educators see those Christians as trying to sneak their religion into the curriculum.

Today's polarized environment produces less dialogue, more sound bites. Terrible sneering insults get thrown at one side or the other. Few attempt to gain mutual understanding. Many launch polemics dedicated to proving the other side wrong.

I've grown deeply concerned about this divide between faith and science. I'm concerned for our society. Are we becoming like the people of Babel, using knowledge to build wonderful towers to our own glory, without God? The more capable we are, the higher we may build our towers. The higher the towers, the more devastating their collapse. Spiritual pride may be difficult to test scientifically, but it is nonetheless real and terribly destructive.

If our civilization is built on science, and most of the people doing science are determined to scoff at God, then I fear for our civilization. I'm just as concerned for what happens among Christians. God created human beings as creatures who explore their world, learning all they can. Watch a baby experiment with sight, taste, and touch. Babies are fantastic learning machines from the day they are born. Ideally, that learning stretches outward through their lives. God made us that way.

When human societies turn their backs on knowledge of the outside world, they stagnate. It has happened more than a few times in history for religious and nonreligious motives. It doesn't turn out well. People who live in ingrown, stagnant societies can't fulfill their God-given destinies. They grow frustrated by the limits that cut them off from growth and learning. They look for someone to blame. Anger and resentment come to dominate their worldview.

Is it possible today's Christian church could become like that? I don't think it could for long. The church has the Bible and the Holy Spirit—life-giving and inspiring. The Bible is a book of love, and love impels us to engage with everything around us. Only by disregarding the fundamental truths of the Bible can you cut yourself off from the world.

Nevertheless, in the short term I feel concern. If we dig a wide ditch between the world of faith and the world of science, we will find ourselves much the poorer for it.

All truth belongs to God, and science is a powerful way of gaining truth. If it weren't, our airplanes wouldn't fly, our cell phones would never connect, and our cancer-taming drugs would heal nothing. We need science not only for airplanes and cell phones and cancer-taming drugs but also for its contact with reality in God's wonderful creation. Christians cut off from science are in trouble spiritually as well as materially.

———————

This book is about men and women whose lives join science and faith. All of them are scientists, trained at the highest levels. All of them are serious and Bible-believing Christians. Unlike so many in our polarized world, they have high regard for both science and the Bible as sources of truth. Their ambition is to bring both sides together.

Which is not to say that they agree with one another. In fact, they have widely varying views. Our eleven scientists provide a good sample of the whole spectrum of Christian beliefs about evolution and creation.

1. *Young earth creationists*, who believe that the world is less than ten thousand years old and that Noah's flood explains most of the geology and fossil distribution that we see today. They also insist that the species of life are not all cousins but were created separately.
2. *Intelligent design creationists*, most of whom believe that the earth is billions of years old but that evolution cannot explain the development of life. Some intelligence must have intervened.
3. *Evolutionary creationists*, who believe that God created life, using evolution. They believe that all creatures are cousin to each other and that the process of variation and selection produces gradual change over millions of years.

Along with their varied understandings of the history of the earth, these scientists vary in their interpretations of Scripture.

The subject of human origins is hot, and Christians get as hot as anybody. You can't look it up on the Internet without hearing one side or the other declaring somebody a heretic or an ignoramus.

I have chosen to profile people who hold strong opinions but aren't quick to condemn others. Some of them admit to seeing weaknesses in their own arguments. Fundamentally, they take seriously the reality that we, the human race, are still learning. Our understanding is partial.

And that understanding must be filled out through ever deeper study of the Bible and of the world God made. These are the "two books" of God's revelation. Those who study both books, seeking truth, stand in the middle of the rift that tries to pull the Bible and the cosmos apart.

I call this book *The Adam Quest*. By that I do not mean the fast-moving search to identify the first human beings through the study of human-like fossils (like Lucy) and more recently through extrapolations of data from human DNA that suggest humanity first developed as an African tribe of perhaps ten thousand individuals.

Those searches are very specific, but I am engaged with a much broader search. By the Adam Quest I mean the attempt to understand where we come from. Adam is the father of all humanity. The search for him is a search for our roots. Metaphorically, he stands for everything in our deepest history.

The Adam Quest involves astrophysics—how did the earth come to be a planet that could sustain life? The search involves geology, especially when considering Noah's flood. It involves paleontology, the hybrid between geology and biology that studies fossils and thus the historical development of life. It involves physics, to tell the age of the earth and to study the molecular forces at work in the cell. It involves biology, to study the living creatures, and biochemistry, to study DNA and proteins and all the extraordinary complexities of the cell. I'm sure I have left out some disciplines. All science gets involved in this attempt to understand our origins, to make historical sense of ourselves.

And, of course, other, nonscientific disciplines join the quest. Biblical studies come first. It is joined by philosophy, which helps us untangle the arguments. (The philosophy of science is particularly valuable, helping explain what science can and can't do.)

Each discipline makes important contributions to the Adam Quest, but unfortunately, each expert sees the quest from only one point of view. Each person's specialization limits his or her ability to see the whole picture. A world-famous biologist may know no more about geology than I do. Even within a single field, each scientist is really an expert only on a very small piece. A microbiologist may know one process of protein formation; he probably knows very little about another.

None of these scientists is truly a Bible scholar, however much they may have read and studied the Bible. Of those I profile, the only one with any trained expertise in biblical texts is John Polkinghorne. The rest, when they say anything about how to read Genesis, are relying on secondhand information. I interviewed several specialists in fields of biblical studies and philosophy, and I read many more, but for the sake of simplicity I am sticking to scientists here.

My point is that the Adam Quest is a team effort. Each person sees it from his or her small area of knowledge. When it comes to each other's fields of knowledge, they can hardly even argue with each other, and when they argue with each other about broader issues, they are not really experts. We can grow in understanding our roots only as we share knowledge together and work together—through debate sometimes—to put the pieces together.

Some will claim that there is nothing to argue about. The Bible settles it, some say; only the details remain. Others take the opposite point of view: science has definitively shown how life developed on earth, and everything else must adjust to fit. To these I can only say that I don't think it's that simple. The lives of the scientists I have profiled suggest that it's not.

As you read about their lives, I hope the Adam Quest will be humanized for you, indeed Christianized. I don't think it's possible to encounter these individuals without knowing them to be devout, Bible-believing Christians who are extremely knowledgeable. There are no fools, knaves, or heretics here. I have found them to be extremely fascinating personalities. They are very smart and very highly trained. I like them all. And their stories are often fascinating.

When you see the Adam Quest from many points of view, your understanding is bound to broaden. You'll grasp better why one person is convinced one way and someone else in another way. You'll understand the points of decision. You may become clearer in your own mind about which perspective you trust.

I have deliberately tried not to declare anybody right or anybody wrong. I lack the authority to do that, and I don't think it would be terribly helpful if I did. Lots of books try to answer all these questions authoritatively. Somehow, though, the questions keep popping up.

My approach has been to find first-rate scientists with different points of view and let them tell their own stories—stories of faith and stories of science. All of them live at the center of the rift, trying to hold faith and science together under God.

One word of advance warning is necessary. In profiling these scientists I have started with three young earth creationists, gone on to those believing in intelligent design, and finished with evolutionary creationists. I group them together because I think they round out each other's points of view. By encountering several young earth creationists, for example, you get a good overall portrait of the young earth creationist perspective.

The downside of grouping these scientists together is that you might find yourself tempted to throw the book across the room if you get repeated doses of a point of view you dislike. If so, I can only urge patience. It's good to understand those with whom you disagree—and all points of view will be presented in due course.

You can choose to skip around. I think, however, that you will get the most from this book if you take the chapters in the order presented.

2 Kurt Wise

A Warrior for Truth

Kurt Wise was born in Rochelle, Illinois, a small town surrounded by fertile, flat farmland. Neither of his parents attended college, though his father was general manager and editor of the local weekly newspaper. They lived on a large wooded property out of town. A solitary child, Wise had a tree house where he liked to go and think or read.

Despite being raised by parents he loved and admired, in a rural Midwest to whose values he still clings, Wise had a miserable childhood. He was short, too smart for his own good, and badly picked on at school. "I wanted to be like everybody else, but early on I realized I was heading for something very different. People would mock me for the way I was speaking. I tried to not learn. I tried to be dumb." Wise recalls a school field trip to a local mental institution where he "saw a few kids just like me—intense, quiet, alone, picked on." He identified with them.

He took refuge in hobbies, many introduced by his father. On his college applications Wise listed thirty-six hobbies and collections, including beekeeping and taxidermy. His interest in fossils began in kindergarten, when he found the fossil of a small mollusk while waiting for the bus. Noting his excitement, his father gave him the Golden Book on fossils and took him to the pit where gravel for local farm roads was mined. "I found hundreds, thousands of fossils over the years," says Wise.

Wise's father was an unconventional thinker. Years later he quit the news business to become economic developer for their town. His very successful approach was to "look for whatever you perceive to be your greatest problem. That will be your greatest success." Rochelle was a crossing for two transcontinental railroads. Everybody complained about the trains, which were noisy and constantly impeded traffic. Wise's father built an observation platform for train enthusiasts—Wise's Folly—and made it a stopping place for hobbyists. A tourist industry was launched.

For Wise, such an approach shimmered like a distant, unreachable light. "My father was bright, wise, and practical. I prefer to live in the completely theoretical." At the age of eight Wise discovered solipsism all by himself. "How do I know that tree is really there? How do I know that I exist?" Aware that none of his friends or family would be able to relate, he kept his questions to himself. Over the next year those questions grew into an existential crisis. Wise says he convinced himself that he should commit suicide. "All I know for sure is the existence of evil. I should commit suicide, to destroy either evil, or nothing. I didn't tell my parents; they don't exist. And why would I leave a note? I wasn't killing myself to get out of the world or to avoid pain." It was a purely philosophical dilemma to be solved by existential means—a nine-year-old version of Camus.

Would he really have killed himself? We will never know because on Palm Sunday he went to Sunday school, where his teacher invited him to commit his life to Christ.

The teacher pushed his Bible across the table to Wise, then used it to guide him through the Romans road, a series of verses in the New Testament book of Romans that offers a simple version of gospel truth.

Wise checked off the verses having to do with universal sin and with death as the wages of sin. ("Yes—suicide.") But when the teacher introduced Romans 5:8, God's love expressed in Christ's sacrificial death, Wise had an epiphany. His desire to do away with evil—even by suicide —suggested that more than evil existed. "If evil is all that exists, it wouldn't desire its own destruction." Suddenly the great exchange, Christ accepting the burden of evil in order to make evil good, made perfect sense to him.

He remembers it as a moment of intellectual awe rather than emotional release. "There's no doubt about it, I'm yours. I'm a believer in a philosophical sense." He committed himself to Jesus. He would not commit suicide. The Bible literally saved his life.

Although Wise's parents regularly attended their fundamentalist Baptist church, they were not heavily involved; his father was not baptized until years later. Wise himself became active through youth group. He later served in Awana, a Bible-based Christian youth program. Still, he continued to think his own lonely thoughts.

In the eighth grade, he prepared a grand science fair project on evolution. He planned to use his hobbies—stuffed birds and fossils—to illustrate the development of life on a staircase of geological time. "I took out both books on evolution from the school library. Then I took out both books on evolution from the city library." But somewhere in the process he began to wonder how evolution fit with the Bible. He couldn't quite square Genesis 1 with what he knew of life's development. Even if the "days" were long periods of time, the order would be wrong.

This question festered until his sophomore year in high school when he decided on a great test. He sneaked out of school and secretly bought a Bible. Under a sleeping bag, by flashlight, he began going through the Bible and carefully cutting out any passage that he would have to eliminate if evolution were true. He took more than a year to do it. "The answer was obvious, but I perceived it as a battle between the Bible and what I loved. I stretched it out. I didn't want to end the process, though I knew what was coming. The only thing I had was school and particularly science. It was my life. I had no idea that evolution was a theory that could be cast out while still accepting science."

When he came to the end of the Bible, he was confronted by Revelation 22:19: "If anyone takes words away from this book of prophecy, God will take away from him his share in the tree of life and in the holy city." He was shaking. "I realized the significance of what I had been doing. I had taken words out of the Bible from beginning to end." When he lifted up the Bible, he had removed so much that the book fell apart in his hand.

He didn't tell anybody about the experiment, but his direction was absolutely clear. "I remembered my Sunday school teacher pushing his Bible across the table for me. I had met Christ through the Bible, saving my life. I couldn't reject the Bible." It was a tragic choice, however. He thought it meant giving up science, his only refuge from the cruelties of life.

Days later, his church youth group went on an "advance" to Normal, Illinois. They were bused to a gymnasium, where a man stood up to say, "I'm a scientist. I'm a Christian. I'm a creationist. I don't believe in evolution."

By the time he entered the University of Chicago, more than a year later, Wise had read everything he could find in creation science literature. "I was a young earth creationist not because of the evidence but because of my faith. I was a creationist because that was the position of the Word of God, and the Word of God was true. No amount of evidence could have the least amount of effect on me. No one would be able to sway me at all."

As miserably lonely as he had been throughout his childhood, being at the University of Chicago was worse. For the first time in his life, he encountered people intellectually more advanced than himself. The university's remorseless competition and high expectations were devastating to him. Nevertheless, he staunchly pursued his calling.

"I went to college as an evangelist. I'm going to convert the University of Chicago, using creationism as a mechanism." Every lunch and dinner at his dormitory cafeteria, six days a week, two hours a day, Wise went looking for a debate. Most days he found it. The table he regularly occupied attracted such a crowd, Wise says, that his roommate went there to meet girls.

One fourth-year geology student debated him many times. He was an evangelical Christian, president of the InterVarsity Christian Fellowship group on campus. "First quarter he brought his own arguments. The second quarter he brought arguments from his geology professors. The third quarter he brought grad students and professors themselves." On the day of his graduation this student searched for and found Wise, thanking him for an incredible year. "I've learned so much," he said.

"I have no evolutionary arguments left," Wise's debate partner continued. "Nevertheless, I'm going to continue being an evolutionist."

Wise sank to his knees and cried, he says. *I won every battle*, he told himself. *Yet I'm not even able to convince a Christian of creationism. What is wrong?* "Then it was as though God slapped me. 'When did you open your Bible?' What an idiot I am! I never used what led me to faith. It had nothing to do with the data."

After that, Wise lost interest in creationist apologetics, especially as he began to realize that many of the creationist evidences from his reading were wrong. "At first I thought it was ignorance." As he learned more, though, he became convinced that the mistakes in creationist literature were willful. Eventually, he sought out leading creationists such as Henry Morris and Duane Gish to complain about arguments presented in their talks. "I was angry. I had been lied to." During a two-hour meeting with Gish, he says, he got Gish to admit that what he was telling audiences was wrong. "Then one week later I heard him saying the same thing [that he had admitted to Wise was wrong] in public." Wise concluded that for many creationists the end justifies the means. For them, "it doesn't matter if what you say is true. It matters if it brings people to the right conclusion."

Saying such things did not endear Wise to other creationists, nor has it since then. He probably has the best scientific credentials of all young earth creationists. But his truth telling grates on others.

"I have this deep desire to know the truth," he says, "and to fight for truth. In elementary school, I would never say anything unless the teacher said something wrong. Then, to my horror, I would raise my hand and confront." His father maintained a similar vigilance through his newspaper, exposing corruption in a way that sometimes led people to threaten his life. When his son heard anything he considered to be a lie, he had to "attack and destroy." This impulse was impossible to control. "It's stronger than I am."

On the other hand, he felt no need to argue with his biology and geology professors at the University of Chicago. He was at school to learn everything they could teach him. He felt only the need to witness to his faith, which included his commitment to creationism. Most of his professors knew what he stood for, and it was they who wrote letters of recommendation for graduate school—particularly for Harvard University's geology department, where Wise sought to work with a famous evolutionary paleontologist, Stephen Jay Gould.

———————

In 1981 Gould was one of the most famous scientists in the world. A student of snails, he and Niles Eldredge introduced the idea of *punctuated equilibrium* in evolution, sometimes jokingly referred to as "evolution by jerks." (Gould said the alternative view, that evolution moves slowly and gradually, was "evolution by creeps.")[1]

Two years before Wise applied to work with him, Gould published a famous paper on spandrels, which elegantly introduced the idea that evolution sometimes produced important new features in organisms as collateral accidents rather than as the direct result of natural selection. He was a wonderful writer and lecturer, daring in his innovative thinking and unafraid of goring sacred cows. Although fiercely opposing creationism, Gould was not a narrow naturalist. He valued the contributions of philosophers and moralists; he promoted the idea of *nonoverlapping magisteria* to suggest that other forms of knowledge, including religion, contributed to areas where science had nothing to say.[2]

Wise had long dreamed of going to Harvard—so much so that he feared he would choose to go there even if it were the wrong place for him. His University of Chicago professors, who knew Gould, suggested he apply. Wise assumed they would tell Gould about his creationist beliefs, which seemed likely to disbar him.

Even so, to protect himself against his own desires, he decided he would go to Harvard only if Gould called him personally, offering a full ride and urging him to come. A letter or a call from someone else would not be sufficient. Wise needed reassurance that God was calling him to Harvard.

He was driving overnight with one of his professors, Dave Raup, a paleontologist who studied the extinction of dinosaurs, when Raup raised a subject that was worrying him. "I don't know if we did the right thing. We decided not to tell Steve you are a creationist."

Wise was horrified. He had not wanted to be deceptive. But deciding that his professors knew better than he, he let it lie.

At one thirty in the morning, he heard the dormitory phone ring in the hallway. Gould himself was on the line. "I've called to ask you, what can I do to persuade you to come to Harvard?"

Wise fell down, stunned. When he found his voice, he said, "You have done everything you need to do. I have no choice."

Months later, when school was set to begin, Wise arrived at Harvard in the middle of the night, having dropped his younger sister at Bob Jones University. Gould, a night owl, was still up. When he realized who Wise was, he began screaming at him. Sometime during the summer, he had learned that Wise was a creationist. He felt deceived and betrayed.

Over eight years at Harvard, though, Wise became quite friendly with Gould. Wise took classes in business, fractal geometry, and mycology, subjects that had no obvious relationship to his subject of study. This eclecticism appealed to Gould, who was an aficionado of the New York Yankees, Gilbert and Sullivan, science fiction, and Renaissance architecture.

Wise discussed creationism with Gould, who responded that "if what you are saying is true, then the Bible's story about a flood may be true, and that God who punished sin is likely still alive. He would not be happy with me. As a consequence, I can't go there." Those last words became Gould's standard comeback whenever Wise introduced creationist ideas.

At one point Wise informed Gould that he had just made Gould's own idea of punctuated equilibrium into a creationist theory that explained more data than Gould's approach. Gould simply said, "I can't go there."

Only once did Wise see spiritual openness. Walking across campus, he happened on Gould sitting on the steps of the Museum of Comparative Zoology, where he had his offices. Gould was staring into space, and Wise sensed that something was very wrong. Without a word he took a seat beside him and waited, praying for wisdom about whether and when to speak. Finally, Gould said, "I've just come back from the doctor. I have cancer, and I am going to die." He had paused on the steps, apparently, to pull himself together before telling his wife and kids. *Stephen Jay Gould's heart is wide open*, Wise realized with astonishment.

Wise spoke to him for some time. He says he has no idea what he said or what impact it had on Gould. That was Saturday.

On Wednesday they met for a weekly gathering, twelve of Gould's advisees around a big table. Each week Gould opened with an interesting tidbit, often humorous. This time he pulled out a letter.

"Dear Professor Gould," he read. The letter was from a Christian, warning him that if he did not accept Jesus as his personal Savior he would go to hell. "I have begun to pray," the letter said, "that you will contract cancer and die."

Gould looked up at his graduate students, who, except for Wise, had no idea why he was reading a letter from a crank. "Today," he said, "his prayer is answered."

"My desire was to shrivel up and disappear below the table," Wise remembers. "I was the only Christian in that group. It was the era of Jim Bakker. [When some scandal appeared in the news] grad students would ask me, 'Why did you do that?' They identified me with Christianity. I knew they would ask me, 'How could you write that letter?'

"That was my first thought. My second thought, I imagined my arms becoming infinitely long, going out the door and into the mailbox and through the entire mail system, finding that person's throat and strangling him.

"Don't you understand that Stephen Jay Gould is not your enemy? That he is not irredeemably lost? What if that letter had closed his heart for the very last time? God forbid. I loved Stephen Jay Gould. Unspeakable evil had been done with that letter. The Bible tells us to love our enemies. How can you give up on anyone?"

Gould survived that cancer and lived another twenty years. Though they remained friendly, Wise never caught him in another moment of vulnerability.

———

Harvard was a happier place for Wise because, for the first time in his life, he found a church fellowship where he belonged. He felt warmly accepted in a small Baptist congregation outside Boston, and it was there he met his wife, Marie.

After the rigors of Chicago, Harvard's academics seemed extremely slack to Wise, even while his fellow grad students were ridiculously ambitious and competitive. He loved the freedom to study, however, pursuing his work in his own time and his own way. "I love sitting in the library. I could do it all my life."

His dissertation was a statistical study of accumulated fossil data, "an estimation of true taxonomic duration from fossil occurrence data." It asked the question, "Given our actual fossil record, how can we estimate when these organisms actually began to exist and when they became extinct?" After Wise presented his work, one of his peers said, according to Wise, "It's obvious this work had to be done. We see that now, but we would never have done it. Your creationist worldview made you see things differently."

Otherwise he put his creationism on hold while he studied. "I wasn't contributing positively. I was only criticizing." He became known in creationist circles as a gadfly. When the time came for his graduation, he wrote to Henry Morris, asking for a job at the Institute for Creation Research. The "father of scientific creationism," as Morris is sometimes called, wrote back to recommend that Wise stay in secular academia, since "you seem to have more love for unbelievers than for believers."

Wise felt increasing doubts about his long-term ambition to teach at a university, however. Christian colleges would be academic suicide for someone in his field, but "the Lord began to impress them on me." With little experience of Christian colleges, Wise wrote blind inquiries. ("And I suppose my letter of recommendation would not be a recommendation for those places?" Gould asked.) Only two schools expressed interest. In the end, only Bryan College interviewed and then offered a job.

——————

On a hill above Dayton, Tennessee, the town where the famous 1925 Scopes trial took place, sits tiny Bryan College. The college was started by local townspeople in commemoration of William Jennings Bryan, the politician who opposed Clarence Darrow at the trial.

When Wise arrived, the school had recently been threatened with extinction. Enrollment had crashed, and the administration had been forced to eliminate tenure, fire half the faculty, and cut the number of majors. A new president managed to stabilize finances, and as he began to rebuild, Wise was his first hire. The vision was to turn Bryan into the premier creationist research institute in the world.

Wise ambitiously named the institute he launched as the Center for Origins Research and Education (CORE). He developed a class on origins and began his own research program. Living near campus, he and his wife welcomed students to their home. "Most of the kids I clicked with were nonscience majors." During most of his seventeen years at Bryan, Wise was the sole CORE employee; only in Wise's last few years did biologist Todd Wood and a lab assistant join.

Wise does not seem to have chafed against the lack of funding for staff or laboratories. He could do his work, which was primarily theoretical and required no labs, and he could focus on the wider community of creationists. He wanted them to work together toward a grand universal theory (GUT) comparable to evolution in its scale and scope.

"I have insisted," Wise says, "that I am not an antievolutionist. I am a creationist. My life goal is to create a model that explains the world." While Genesis gives a broad outline of the history of creation, the stories need filling in with scientific detail. For example, where did the water for Noah's flood come from, to raise the sea level so high? What caused the waters to rise? In what way did the Flood affect the geological features we see today, like canyons and caves?

With a creationist model that explained more of the world better, "[evolutionists] won't have any choice but to jump ship," Wise insists.

Wise longed to study fossils, he says, but first needed a synthetic theory for biology and geology, the two fields that come together in paleontology. He put fossils aside and tried to lead creation scientists in working together.

The so-called Gang of Six came together at his prodding. Their goal was to develop a unified understanding of the geology of Noah's flood.

Scattered in many locations, they were qualified scientists with expertise in relevant disciplines. Wise believed a comprehensive theory could be built out of their separate work.

In 1994 the Gang of Six published a paper sketching what they believed to be the true history of a young earth formed mainly by the Flood.[3] "Catastrophic plate tectonics" suggests that the Flood was caused by a rupture in the earth's crust, causing the leading edge of continents to dive down deep into the molten mantle thousands of times faster than plates currently move—at a speed of meters per second, rather than millimeters per year. The resulting catastrophe transformed the earth's climate and raised the sea floor, thus pushing the sea level above the highest mountains. In the cataclysmic turbulence of the Flood, all living creatures (except those in the ark) were drowned and buried. In a year's time most of the geologic column—hundreds of millions of years of sediment and deposition, in traditional geology—and the vast majority of all fossils were laid down. The theory suggests that we find different fossil species in different geological strata because various ecozones were reached by the floodwaters in sequential stages. For example, mammals were laid down last because they lived at higher altitudes far from the coastlines where floodwaters first reached. After the sea floor returned to a lower level, massive continental floods carved canyons, including the Grand Canyon.

In Wise's 2002 book *Faith, Form, and Time*, an attempt to lay out a comprehensive creationist vision, he writes that "while young-age creation geology is superior to alternate models in a number of areas, it is admittedly weak in a variety of others. Much research is needed to provide adequate young-age creationist reinterpretations of these issues."[4] Wise knows that catastrophic plate tectonics only throws out a story line; there are very few details. At numerous points he calls for more research, noting data that the theory cannot yet fully explain.

Conventional geologists and paleontologists have shown no detectable interest in the theory, except to heap it with scorn. (How, for example, did vast numbers of extinct trilobites get buried in the lower flood sediments, yet not a single one managed to swim or tumble through the floodwaters to die in a higher layer of mud?)

Wise sees the theory as a success, explaining many geological features that are problematic for conventional geology. What troubles him most, he says, is that nobody has carried on the research. The Gang of Six split up, and one member has become Wise's "deep-seated enemy" for reasons Wise fails to understand. Almost twenty years after its publication, the theory is scientifically sterile. Wise describes himself as "shocked and dejected" by the lack of follow-up.

Wise also sought a grand universal theory for creationist biology. In 1990 he offered a paper introducing what he called *baraminology*.[5] *Baramins* are the "created kinds" of Genesis. Baraminology attempts to identify, through various scientific tests, what creatures God originally created. Most young earth creationists believe that there has been super-rapid diversification of species by unknown means since the Flood. For example, creationists suspect that God's created kind was the dog. It has since diverged into various species such as wolf, coyote, and dingo, as well as dachshund and Great Dane.

Baraminology differs from conventional biology in that it perceives unbridgeable differences between the baramins, while evolution posits common ancestry for all life. Creationist biologists don't deny the genetic and biochemical similarities between all creatures, but they see them as a testament to a common designer, who used the same basic tools in each of his creatures.

Wise focused on baraminology because "systematics is the first thing you need in a field. You need to name things and distinguish them from each other." Evolutionists see continuity everywhere, but creationists have an eye for discontinuity. To develop this vision, they need a naming system that accurately captures the distinctions between the creatures—that can distinguish between created difference and the diversification of species that creationists believe has happened since Noah.

During the 1990s, Wise encouraged a small group of biology graduate students to work on these problems. His role was catalytic; he wanted to turn baraminology over to them. In 1996 or 1997—memories diverge—those biologists met together for the first time at Bryan College. They subsequently formed the Creation Biology Society. One of them, Todd Wood, became the de facto leader of creationist biology, especially baraminology. The goal was to create a scientific enterprise that parallels conventional biology, with its own journals and meetings.

Like creation geology, creation biology remains in its infancy. It has an annual meeting and has developed peer-reviewed journals, but research is based on data published by evolutionary biologists. Almost no laboratory experiments are done because there are no laboratories with advanced equipment in which to do them.

In Wise's first decade at Bryan, he offered conferences bringing together the best minds in creationism. Building year to year, he planned a superconference in the year 2000, inviting fifty people he believed to be the best young earth creationist scientists in the world.

Then, in February 2000, a fire broke out in his office and badly damaged the entire academic building. Wise's personal library was destroyed, along with the research data he had been accumulating. "It knocked me out for a very long time, and some of it I never recovered."

CORE had to operate from temporary quarters while the building was restored. The college pulled back from supporting the 2000 conference, and it had to be canceled.

The fire not only threw Wise's work into disarray; it seemed to jar his confidence. Looking around at the creationist movement, he saw discord everywhere. Organizational rivalries were vicious. Splits and lawsuits were widely publicized. "A creationist learns how to fight. Now you want them to get along with people?"

If creation science were to make progress, its scientists would have to collaborate. Wise saw that he was ill suited to fostering that. All his life he had found it difficult to build positive relationships.

He began to rethink his efforts. He had tried to foster cooperation through such efforts as the Gang of Six and the Creation Biology Society. He had helped encourage a creationist geology program at Cedarville University in Ohio, and there were talks of starting a program at Master's College in California. "I asked myself, suppose we succeed at half a dozen Christian colleges. That's good, but not good enough." The problem was, too few students wanted to study creationist science. They would come only if their pastors had a vision for it. "We needed to impact pastors."

Wise talked to seminaries. In 2006, after a lengthy search, he was hired at Southern Baptist Theological Seminary in Louisville, Kentucky, to establish a center for science and theology. The seminary's president, Al Mohler, had an expansive vision that included a center for law and government and one for the arts. Wise has never formally studied theology, but never lacking for intellectual confidence, he dove into the literature of science and Christianity. He was appalled at the lack of a conservative Christian voice in the academic literature. His center had no money, not even to allow him to attend meetings, but he developed courses and worked on writing textbooks to accompany them.

Then, facing a financial shortfall, the seminary pulled the plug on all three centers. With little warning, Wise found himself looking for another job. His place at Bryan had long since been filled. He was, he feared, unemployable. "There's no respect for young earth creationism in the Christian world. You'll find more acceptability at Harvard than at a Wheaton."

Creationist organizations didn't want him because of his reputation as a critic. By June, with his contract ending, he began to consider a career in landscaping. It would be a humbling end for someone who says, "I was groomed to be one of the giants of science."

————————

Eight o'clock on a Thursday morning, a dozen students in shorts and T-shirts straggle into their biology classroom. The room's slate tables and gas outlets, its glass cases filled with skulls and deer antlers, might be found in science classrooms anywhere, as might the yawning students. Truett-McConnell is a small Southern Baptist college in the Georgia Appalachians, only recently turned from a two-year to a four-year school.

Kurt Wise stands before the class, a tall man with thick gray hair and a middle-aged paunch, wearing a dark green shirt and a green-and-yellow Day-Glo tie. This class is for nonscience majors, "devotional biology," as Wise calls it. His topic is God as communicator.

The curriculum, which Wise developed, is organized around attributes of God, finding evidences of God's nature written in the created world. For God as communicator Wise looks to the omnipresence of DNA in all organisms. DNA is sometimes called the "blueprint of life," Wise says. "A naturalist must believe this statement. But it turns out not to be true."

We are learning that DNA plays a limited role, Wise tells his students. For example, frog eggs that have their nuclei removed (with the DNA) will still divide and replicate themselves ten times. For example, the human body is a community of organisms, with valuable parasites whose contribution we are only beginning to understand.

Wise ranges over a variety of material, making the point that DNA is only one aspect of who we are, not the sum total. "DNA alone can do nothing. . . . The people who discovered DNA were naturalists. . . . Watson [one of DNA's discoverers] promulgated this lie [that DNA is the blueprint of life] in our society, and society has bought it. The church has bought it. . . . I believe a significant amount of information is coming from the soul and spirit."

Nevertheless, Wise soon turns to admiring DNA, a mile-long molecule that "could code entire libraries." DNA duplicates itself and checks for accuracy with amazing speed. "This is so cool!" Wise exclaims in delight. "There is no more efficient way to carry information or to copy information than this design."

He compares DNA's coding to the way languages work. Language, Wise says, only comes from communicating beings. And so, God's imprint is visible in all life, as though each organism's DNA represented a tag saying, "Made by God."

After mandatory chapel, three students turn up for a class on origins. "My first love was fossils," Wise tells them and then describes the Gang of Six and catastrophic plate tectonics. Racing through an explanation of the makeup of the earth—core, mantle, crust—he gives several examples of how catastrophic plate tectonics explains geological facts that confound conventional science.

After lunch, Wise teaches a laboratory class for the devotional biology students, in which they string together beads and magnets in order to get a simplified understanding of mitosis and meiosis—two forms of cell division.

Throughout this day of teaching, Wise's students act cheerful and compliant but not notably engaged. They say very little and ask almost no questions. This reaction might describe many colleges' general studies courses, which students take to fulfill requirements. But it is a far cry from the rigorous, competitive environment that Wise grew up in at the University of Chicago and at Harvard. If there are ardent young creationists here, they are undercover.

Truett is a small school with just seventy students in the 2012 graduating class. It is growing fast since it has become the most theologically conservative of the three Georgia colleges supported by the Southern Baptist Convention. Its president, Emir Caner, has a shaved head and a full beard. Born in Sweden to a Muslim father, he grew up in the United States and converted to Christianity as a youth. He and his brother, Ergun, have been controversial coauthors on Islam.

Just when Kurt Wise was growing desperate for a job, Emir Caner contacted him. Caner was rebuilding Truett around the twin pillars of young earth creationism and missions. (The lobby of the school's main building, Miller Hall, has a large inscription: "From the very first verse to the very last tribe." On the left are the creation research center and Wise's office. On the right is the world missions center.) Caner wanted to add a science major to the curriculum and asked Wise to head the effort.

Wise loved Caner's educational vision. Making it reality proved to be a hellish job, however. The biology faculty resisted. Several professors left or were fired. "It was much worse than I thought," Wise says, "a terrible struggle."

After three years, the worst was over, and Wise could focus on his long-term aims. He does little or no science research now, though he hopes to get back into it when he sheds some of his administrative burdens. Primarily, he sees another priority. "We have to train a new generation," he says. Developing a new science curriculum is crucial. (He regards present creationist textbooks, mainly developed for homeschoolers, as dreadful.)

Sometimes he speaks proudly of creation science and its achievements. "There are not many of us. We haven't been working at it very long. We don't have money. But we have nevertheless developed a model which is comparable in explanatory power to the conventional model." On the other hand, "I don't think we are going to win. I see no success. Creationism will never be accepted in my lifetime."

He regards himself as a theoretical scientist. "My role is to create the superstructure. Others will put in the windows and doors." The problem is that so little practical young earth creationist science is being done. Few are putting in windows and doors. That is why the next generation is so important. Somehow, more scientists must be trained.

It is very clear that Wise loves science passionately. Creation science is not for apologetic purposes, he insists. Apologetics are the scourge of the church, driving people away from God because they are based on evidence and reason, not faith. Science should give insight into God himself. A beautiful God expresses himself in a beautiful universe. God's attributes are displayed "ubiquitously, abundantly, deeply."

One can learn about these attributes from reading the Bible. "But some people see the Bible as just words and concepts. Science shows it's really there. It's reality. Scientists are trained to see it. That is the scientist's role in the church—reading his creation revelation.

"My role as a Christian and a scientist is to be a priest. I'm to glorify God to the church."

3 Todd Wood

A Simple Truth Seeker

"My grandfather came by the house one day with some old books in his pickup truck. There was a 1934 human anatomy textbook that I claimed for my own. As a nine-year-old kid, I memorized all the bones in the human body. I made up a sign, 'Dr. Todd Wood,' to put on my door. I always knew I was going to be a scientist. When other kids were reading Dr. Seuss, I was reading the *Golden Book of Dinosaurs*."

Rives Junction is an unincorporated village in the heart of Michigan where Todd Wood was born in 1972. A quiet boy and an only child, Wood spent most of his happiest time alone. His father was a truck driver, and the family lived on thirteen acres, a remnant of Wood's great-great-grandfather's farm, bought in the nineteenth century. The nearest neighbor was out of sight, but a short walk through a marsh brought Wood to his grandmother and aunt. Northwest Baptist, a small fundamentalist church his parents had helped start, was at the heart of his life. Many of its members were his relatives.

He attended a Baptist school, K–12, with twenty-five students in his graduating class. Research papers were his joy; he loved going far beyond the teacher's expectations in tracking down extensive sources.

Among the family's collection of books were two having to do with origins: Henry Morris and John Whitcomb's *The Genesis Flood* and *Has Anybody Really Seen Noah's Ark?* by Violet Cummings. These fascinated Wood. In high school he wrote a paper on a news account that got attention in creationist circles. A Japanese fishing boat pulled a creature from the depths that looked, judging from news photos, exactly like an extinct plesiosaur. The story stirred Wood. The suggestion that dinosaurs had not disappeared millions of years ago, but might still exist, excited him. Like reports of an ark surviving on Mount Ararat, it was evidence supporting the Bible.

When Wood was seventeen, his grandfather was diagnosed with cancer. For the first time, "life intruded on my simple little world." His grandfather died during Wood's freshman year in college. He was not a Christian and had not wanted to discuss his lack of faith. "It forced me to think about eternity. What can I do to be a better witness?" Wood emerged with a deeper commitment, one that would stay strong when many of the kids he grew up with veered off the path.

Wood graduated at the top of his high school. He considered two colleges: Liberty University (founded by Jerry Falwell) and the even stricter fundamentalist Bob Jones University (BJU). Accepted at BJU, he hesitated because of stories he had heard about its rigid rules of conduct. Over the phone he asked his admissions counselor to send him a student handbook. The counselor said he could do that only after Wood had signed his letter of commitment. Wood was a very serious, well-behaved teenager, but something in him rebelled against the "trust me" approach. On that basis alone, he decided to attend Liberty.

Liberty University proved to be a wonderful place for Wood. The biology department emphasized field studies, and Wood delighted in the freedom of the woods and waters. He came home for the summer after his first course in botany, seeing the same species blooming in the Michigan woods that he had observed in Virginia one month earlier. The world of biology opened to him. A major research project had him assessing the effects of logging on salamanders in the Blue Ridge Mountains. "It was one thing to read, another to see it in the field."

Quite on his own he discovered a rich vein of creationist publications in the library. Typically, he learned about young earth creationism all by himself. He didn't take a class in origins until near the end of college, and by that time, he says, he could have taught the class.

Scientific creationism as a movement had been born almost thirty years earlier with the publication of *The Genesis Flood*. Henry Morris was a professor of hydraulic engineering fascinated by questions of origins. John Whitcomb was an Old Testament professor who read Genesis literally. Together they updated the writings of George Price, a Seventh-day Adventist schoolteacher and amateur geologist who believed that almost all geological formations worldwide had been laid down in Noah's flood about six thousand years before. Price's ideas attracted limited interest until Morris and Whitcomb subtracted the Adventist references and popularized the material for a wider audience. It was a huge success. An affable figure, Morris helped to found the Creation Research Society (CRS) and later the Institute for Creation Research.

Popular resistance to evolution had a much deeper history, of course. The idea that man and monkeys are related has met a steady stream of humor and invective almost since Darwin. Creation science, however, was an attempt to build a new science on the framework of a literal reading of Genesis. It claimed to be *science*, offering evidence that did not depend on the Bible. The creationist literature Wood discovered featured reports that evolutionary theory could not explain, such as fossilized dinosaur tracks intermingled with human footprints.

Wood learned from noncreationist sources as well. Required to write a research paper for a genetics class, Wood asked permission to study something mentioned in their textbook: mitochondrial Eve. This was a recent development showing that all human mitochondrial DNA can be traced to a single female buried deep in human prehistory. Researching this took Wood deep into evolutionary literature, reading from primary sources. Creationist publications were dismissive of mitochondrial Eve, but Wood wrote a letter to the CRS quarterly suggesting that mitochondrial Eve could be significant and that creationists should pay attention.

He began to realize that not everything he read in creationist literature was reliable. In creationist publications, Wood came across articles critical of some earlier creationist claims. "I got assurance that I wasn't crazy."

Woods loved biology. He expected to teach it in high school, paying off his college debts before perhaps doing graduate studies. When his professors explained that graduate schools would pay *him* to study science, he could hardly believe it. "My self-image is nothing special," he explains. He always had modest expectations for himself.

Still following his plan to teach, he registered for fall classes his senior year at Liberty and encountered a familiar problem. The science faculty and the education faculty would not coordinate their schedules. Wood's final required education class conflicted with his final required biology class. In frustration, he decided on the spot to give up studying education. Walking through the halls of the science department, he pulled grad school inquiry cards off the bulletin board. He applied to just one school, the University of Virginia, to study biochemistry. He was one of five students accepted.

––––––––

On his first day at the University of Virginia, Wood went to a biochemistry lab and encountered a professor "talking about DNA analysis and yaks. I was listening and nodding and thinking to myself, *What do yaks have to do with it?* I'm feeling as though I just fell off the turnip truck, and I'm trying not to show it."

Sometime later he learned that the professor spoke of YAC, yeast artificial chromosome, a manufactured organism that is useful for the study of cloning. "I was completely ignorant of big science and labs of the kind they use. Completely ignorant. I am amazed they didn't just throw me out. I was so overwhelmed.

"When I say God wouldn't put you into grad school and teach you all this stuff if he didn't want you to use it, that's really personal to me," Wood says. "I had no business getting into grad school. I was blown away, socially and emotionally."

He rented an apartment far out of town and realized that, on his budget, he could eat just one meal a day. Usually, that was a frozen dinner he could purchase for $1.25. Sometimes he was so hungry he could not wait for the oven to thaw it all the way: he ate it still cold in the middle.

Wood was not naturally gifted in the laboratory. One of his earliest assignments was to purify a protein. He was given the recipe—two single-spaced pages of steps that needed to be completed in one twenty-four-hour cycle. Once he started the exacting process, he could not leave it or take a break to sleep. In the middle of the night, another grad student wandered into the lab and asked Wood what he was doing. He acted surprised at Wood's answer. "It isn't supposed to be done in the cold room," he said. "Maybe it won't matter." When Wood finished the twenty-four-hour purification process, he found he had produced none of the desired protein. "Who knows where it went? I didn't have a clue."

Only one support kept him together in his utter loneliness and bewilderment: Wayne Hills Baptist Church. He joined the choir. "That church is why I didn't quit."

Also important was a conversation with a friend from Liberty. It was her birthday, and in celebration they went out to eat. A morose Wood told her that he didn't know whether he was going to make it in graduate school. She didn't sympathize. Instead, she reminded him of what he had said when he was accepted: that he got in by a miracle.

"You're right," I told her. "People forget. I had forgotten why I was in grad school." He loved biology, and he loved the Bible. He had gone to Virginia intending to bring them together.

While laboratory experimentation was traumatic for Wood, his love for library research and his mathematical abilities paid off in the classroom, where he did very well. Computational analysis was just beginning to become a significant part of biology, as decoding the genome produced reams of data that required computer analysis. "It clicked. To this day I get a nice little charge of happiness when I see sequence data. I don't know why.

"Some cynical people might say I just wanted to use it for my crazy creationist nonsense. But I was and I remain genuinely interested in molecular evolution and believe it has a lot to offer.

"I was determined to be a student. I didn't want to argue or make a fuss or try to correct the profs. I was there to learn. I wouldn't shy away if confronted, but I did not wave the flag every day. I went in fully aware of the stereotype of creationists as bellicose. I didn't want to be anything like that." His professors, he soon realized, were hardly the enemy; they were brilliant men and women introducing him to a wonderful world where, he discovered, he could thrive.

The first organismal genome sequence—for a bacteria—was published during Wood's first year of graduate school. From there the race was on to sequence more and more organisms. Genome sequences provided not only fascinating data to analyze but also strong evidence for the evolutionary tree of life. A look at the DNA of chimps and humans indicated it was virtually the same. Even humans and bacteria were extraordinarily similar at the molecular level. Traces of common origins were everywhere. For example, humans possess a broken version of a gene that lizards and birds use to produce eggs. Wood remained fully committed to a six-day creation—he says he never doubted it for a minute. But that didn't keep him from recognizing that evolution had powerful attestation.

"Part of the process was abandoning naive apologetic creationism, which I still held on to. Evolution made a lot of sense. There was no conspiracy behind it.

"Doubt never occurred to me. It has always been a challenging puzzle to solve. If Genesis 1–11 is really a historical account, then what does all this data mean? That has always been my approach. I have always been comfortable talking about things, but in the end I am going to say, what is the creationist approach to this?

"The pendulum swing always baffles me." As an example Wood gives the testimony of historian Ronald Numbers, who candidly writes that his faith dissolved when he discovered discrepancies between science and his understanding of the Bible. "Why throw it all out? These are my attempts to make sense of God's eternal truth. I will not pretend that I have the right formula for figuring it out.

"I'm not so interested in what's wrong with [the evolutionists'] idea. I'm more interested in solving the puzzling issues building from Genesis. I don't have all the answers. I approach it with humility."

While enthralled with what he was learning at the University of Virginia, Wood also became an activist participant in the creationist movement. Previously, creation science crept along with the publication of hard-to-find books and journals, plus the occasional conference. The Internet, which took off while Wood was in graduate school, changed all that. It enabled creationists to find each other and create an ongoing discussion.

Wood joined some of the earliest e-mail lists and jumped into the conversation. As a graduate student at a top-ranked school, he helped refine creationist thinking. Wood became a volunteer editor for a CRS newsletter. He met Kurt Wise through the Internet and learned of his interest in baraminology.

Some of the old apologetic arguments didn't hold up, he realized. The fossilized dinosaur tracks mingling with human footprints proved, on further analysis, to be nothing but dinosaur tracks, some smeared. Wood contributed to debunking the living plesiosaur when he unearthed the Japanese technical report. The creature from the deep turned out to be a decaying shark. He wrote an article for the CRS quarterly reporting his findings. When other creationists wrote in to rebut his report, the narrowness of their thinking shocked him.

Many of the creationists' assertions missed the point, he realized, knocking down straw men. More fundamentally, science moved forward not by disproving theories but by advancing better ones. Creationism would win its argument when it demonstrated that it explained God's creation better than an evolutionary model.

How to do that? Only a few months into graduate school he perceived, with a shock, that none of his Internet dialogue partners had answers. He knew as much as anybody. And he still had questions.

The most obvious fact about created life is its extravagant variety, all built from a fundamental similarity at the molecular level. Evolution explained this as the product of gradual variation from some original organism. Creationism explained the same facts as the product of a designer who repeatedly used basic designs. But Wood didn't find the creationists' explanation particularly illuminating. It could be applied to any facts that came along, and it didn't help Wood understand God's creation more deeply. "I want to understand what God is thinking. Why did he make chimps almost the same as humans?"

As he probed for answers, a small e-mail–connected group of biology grad students emerged. They met informally for the first time in 1997 at Bryan College, with Kurt Wise's encouragement.

The group agreed that their first step would be to identify the biological units of God's creation, the created kinds of Genesis 1. They believed that God had created life in certain limited forms, which had since diversified. If they could work backward to those original forms, they would have the basis for understanding similarity and diversity. This basic work, known as *baraminology*, would become Wood's research focal point as a creationist.

First, though, he had to finish his dissertation. When Wood talks of this, his sentences trail off into silence. "It was very, very difficult to do." He had proposed a project in structural biology, but at an academic conference at Carnegie Mellon in Pittsburgh, he noticed a big-name biologist giving a talk. Its title was "suspiciously similar to what I had just proposed." He watched the man go through his slides and realized with a desperate sinking feeling that it was *exactly* the same. He had just been scooped.

He had to come up with a different dissertation. His research had wandered into several areas, and he tried to patch them together into one big idea. The attempt didn't work. His adviser kept sending his papers back to him. "I am too much of a perfectionist. I have to be the best. I couldn't just get it done."

Living near the Shenandoah Valley, Wood often sought solace in the beautiful woods and hills. One day, feeling utterly depressed by the stress of his dissertation, he went for a hike on one of his favorite trails. He spotted a flower he had never seen, growing in a crack in a rock face. Fumbling out his guidebook, Wood found a picture. The flower was called bleeding heart. He was utterly dumbfounded. This was surely a message from God aimed directly at him: a bleeding heart, firmly rooted in the cleft of the rock.

Wood finished his doctoral dissertation ("Theory and Application of Protein Homology") happy to see its completion, though quite dissatisfied with the result. He took a postdoctoral position at Clemson University, part of a team that was decoding the rice genome. The multimillion-dollar grant solidified his dislike for big science. During graduate school, he noted with dismay that his professors seemed to spend much of their time writing grant proposals. At Clemson he lived the high-pressure, long-hours lifestyle that comes with large teams of scientists working within time and budget constraints. Wood remained a solitary character. He loved science when he could explore problems in his own time and in his own way. He didn't like being a laboratory manager.

After a year at Clemson, he did the unthinkable. He applied for a position at tiny Bryan College to work with Kurt Wise. He knew it meant the end of his career in conventional science, yet when Wise offered the position, Wood took it with a sense of grateful calling. Finally, he would have time and opportunity to work at science in the way in which he believed.

There were no big research labs and no million-dollar budgets at Bryan, but a computer was all Wood really needed to do fundamental analysis of created kinds. He began careful statistical analysis of data drawn from published scientific reports. The field of cladistics, developed in the 1960s, drew family trees using detailed descriptions of organisms to compare similarities and differences. These descriptions could be adapted to baraminology. Where cladistics looked for relationship, baraminology looked for difference. Wood hoped to find distinct groupings within a cross section of species; a cluster might represent one of the created kinds of Genesis 1. (Wood's understanding of baraminology is laid out in his 2003 book, *Understanding the Pattern of Life*, coauthored with Megan Murray.)

Wood worked at his analysis with uncontroversial organisms, until he felt ready to tackle the creationist battleground: humans. "People don't care about the evolution of grass," Wood says. "Talk about the evolution of humans, and suddenly, they are paying attention." Using published data from the crania of hominid fossil finds, Wood looked for clusters. Evolution would predict continuity between the various specimens, reflecting a family tree, but young earth creationists would expect to find an unbridgeable gap between *Homo sapiens* and nonhuman species such as apes.

"I found separate clusters, just as I had expected. I was thrilled." Wood wrote a paper for the creationist group Answers in Genesis' online journal. "I expected a hero's welcome."

Just before publication, though, he learned of a new fossil find, *Australopithecus sediba.* Written up extensively in *Science, sediba* would be a great test case, Wood thought, and he decided to add it to his data set. In Wood's analysis, *sediba* proved to be not an intermediate on the family tree, but distinctly in the human grouping. "It's a slam dunk for creation biology. Clearly, there are different kinds" of hominids.

But other creationists did not share his jubilation. "I got a fierce reaction. Responses were breathtaking and disappointing at the same time. I think my ego was the most disappointed. I thought people would be excited. I had showed them that you could tell the difference between humans and nonhumans." Many creationists were intensely uncomfortable, however, with including in the human family a creature that looked so unlike modern humanity.

The experience suggested a basic divergence: many creationists are dedicated to apologetics, which depends on having convincing answers. Wood wants to do science, which is more invested in asking the right questions and following them wherever they lead. "I want to redeem science," Wood says. "I don't want to refute science." Wood believes that the questions he poses based on his reading of Genesis will lead to greater illumination. He doesn't claim to have all the answers. If he did, there would be no room for science.

———

Todd Wood's office at Bryan University is reached through the science museum, a small and eclectic collection of fossils, stuffed animals, dead snakes coiled in bottles, and other science arcana. His office decor is more ironic, containing a small collection of silly tourist memorabilia from a London exhibition on Darwin and a large poster of the skeletons of major vertebrates—mammals, reptiles, fish, birds, and so on—showing how similar their body plans appear. Judging from their skeletons, they look related—which is why Wood displays the poster. He likes to keep his students—and himself—honest.

Anna, a student, approaches Wood to discuss her research project. "Do you have 'R' on your computer?" Wood asks. She has no idea what "R" is—a computer program for analyzing statistical data. He instructs her on downloading it and then walks her through her project. She takes word-for-word notes on her laptop as he talks.

Wood is a dark-haired man of medium height, wearing glasses and a full beard. He has a casual, gentle manner that sometimes allows an offbeat sense of humor to show through. Anna's research involves analyzing the ratios between transitions and transversions, two kinds of genetic mutations. The shape of the DNA helix is more dramatically changed when a transversion occurs, Wood explains to Anna, which prompts the cell to correct it. Thus, fewer transversion mutations are found than transition mutations. However, Wood has noticed that the ratio between the two varies by organism, and he wonders whether this could be a signal for a different created kind. For example, human DNA and Neanderthal DNA have the same ratio, but chimpanzees' ratio is different. On evolutionary grounds, it's hard to imagine why.

In a previous research project, Anna looked at the fossil record of flowering plants. Since young earth creationists believe that most fossils were laid down in Noah's flood, fossilized flowers should nearly represent the original created kinds. The idea for Anna's project is to check whether these created kinds might also show their differences in the ratio of transversions to transitions.

"If you look at all the flowering plants," Wood says, "sunflowers to lilies to oak trees, very different plants, you find that their genes are almost the same. It's challenging. How do we draw the line, and where do we draw it? If we're ignoring 97 percent of the data, does the line mean anything? Evolutionists would say we are grasping at straws. But it's possible that the differences may harbor a signal."

Wood discusses some statistical issues with Anna. For example, "the sample size could be a meaningful problem" as she zeroes in on particular families of flowers. "It's good to be aware of these details so we don't go off and prematurely claim that we have solved the problem of identifying the created kinds."

In 2010, paleontologist Phil Senter published a paper in the *Journal of Evolutionary Biology* using Wood's statistical approach for a purpose Wood would not have contemplated: he showed that dinosaurs are closely related to birds. It was a backhanded compliment to Wood, that his work was taken seriously enough to be critiqued in a mainstream journal and his techniques used to undermine his point of view. In principle Wood is glad to be engaging in that kind of critique; he responded with an article in the same journal, one of the very rare occasions when a creationist has published in a mainstream science journal. Nevertheless, Senter's critique exposed a weakness in Wood's approach.

Wood has grown increasingly frustrated by the methods he has been using to determine created kinds. He had hoped these methods would improve with experience, but problems have not gone away. Anna's project represents an entirely new approach.

Wood joined Bryan's Center for Origins Research and Education (CORE) in 2000 and took over leadership from Kurt Wise in 2006. It has not expanded in that time, but on the other hand, Bryan has not faltered in funding two faculty members and a research assistant, giving them time for research. No other creationist institution makes such a commitment, Wood says. He would love to add more faculty, labs, and grad students, but that takes money and he has no gift for promotion and fund-raising. It must be said that in many ways Bryan's program offers exactly what Wood loves best: a chance to work at his own pace and in his own way, with minimal administration.[1]

Wood and his colleagues at CORE oversee projects like Anna's for a number of students. It's serious scientific research of a kind that many scientists would be surprised to find in a creationist institution. Nevertheless, it's impossible to miss that Wood leads only handfuls of undergraduates without laboratory equipment or funding. Compared to many thousands of research scientists working in high-tech labs to advance understanding according to evolutionary models, it's a peashooter facing the US Army's artillery.

Wood is not daunted. In order to be a young earth creation scientist, you have to be stunningly independent. He is proud that his graduates understand evolution, not just a caricature. In his classes they read Darwin's *On the Origin of Species.* "It's still extremely compelling." Nevertheless, his students remain committed creationists.

"I'm searching for someone willing to help me develop the next generation of baraminology." Apologetic groups like Answers in Genesis keep the creationist faith alive, he says, but producing the next generation of scientists is more problematic.

"Where are the twentysomethings?" Wood knows a few now in graduate school. One of his students just got into a prominent university after a long struggle. ("He struggled because he came from Bryan, where creationist crackpots are running around, and we don't have whiz-bang lab equipment.")

Science is partly a numbers game. It takes lots of trained scientists poking their fingers into lots of different problems to make a breakthrough. Creation biology has enough intriguing findings to give him encouragement, Wood says, but it still lacks an overall coherence. "We need our own Darwin."

The launch of BioLogos, a Christian organization begun by the

Human Genome Project's Francis Collins, has changed the terms of debate among Christians, Wood notes. He is intrigued by the organization's willingness to promote evolutionary creationism while admitting it doesn't have all the answers, especially regarding Genesis.

"I'm beginning to think the war [between Christians with different views on evolution] is detrimental to the church. We all have enormous unanswered questions, whether scientific or biblical. We all see through a glass darkly." That does not imply that he is backing away from his young earth creationism. On the contrary, he believes that the theological core of the Bible—creation, fall, and redemption—hangs on a young earth creationist interpretation. And he looks forward to seeing God's Word vindicated. The Bible often tells of times when God's word seemed laughable, Wood notes—when the aged Abraham and Sarah were told they would have a child and when Jesus said that Lazarus was asleep. "When God is speaking, all bets are off. You think you know how the world works, but you have no idea."

Ending the war will involve repentance on all sides, he thinks. "I can't make somebody else repent of what he is doing wrong. I can only repent of what I am doing wrong. If I do that publicly enough, maybe I will inspire others. The quest stops being about saving the church and exposing heresy. It starts being about serving the Creator, which it was always supposed to be."

Talk about repentance makes some young earth creationists suspicious of Wood, as he knows very well. "This is a culture war. There is no room for me to give aid and comfort to the enemy. I am just trying to be fair, but many view me with a great deal of suspicion.

"It can be discouraging, but I try not to let it be discouraging." Wood gives a wan smile. "It would be great if the war ended at Bryan College."

4 Georgia Purdom
A Passion to Teach

The handsome front gate of the Creation Museum near Cincinnati, Ohio, is adorned with cutout metal dinosaurs. A wide plaza at the museum entrance features a twenty-foot model of a dinosaur. Highway billboards advertise the museum with pictures of dinosaurs.

"It is a measure of the museum's daring," a *New York Times* reviewer wrote, "that dinosaurs and fossils—once considered major challenges to belief in the Bible's creation story—are here so central."[1]

In the common understanding, dinosaurs stand for just what the Creation Museum exists to contradict: a millions-year-old past. Yet the Creation Museum says, loud and clear, "we have dinosaurs." Inside the museum is a large stand-alone exhibit devoted just to dinosaurs. As you go through the museum, dinosaurs show up far more often than any other signifier—more than Adam and Eve, for instance, or Noah's ark.

Anyone imagining the Creation Museum as a joke run by backwoods hillbillies is bound to be surprised. Set in a large modern building a short drive from the Cincinnati airport, the museum is a highly professional educational experience, comparable to the best big-city natural history museums.

Like any good modern museum, the Creation Museum aims to communicate with the masses—and clearly, the masses like dinosaurs. Dinosaurs possess a majestic but homely grandeur, unlike, say, trilobites, the equally extinct arthropods that once teemed in our seas. You can't build a popular museum around trilobites.

Young earth creationists have problems fitting dinosaurs into their story. The rocks from which dinosaur fossils come are millions of years old, according to a wide variety of scientific analyses. There's also the problem of why some dinosaurs display sharp flesh-tearing carnivore teeth, since young earth creationists believe that God created nothing but vegetable-eating animals. And how did dinosaurs fit inside Noah's ark? And why did dinosaurs disappear after the Flood? (Some creationists think that stories of dragons reflect the existence of dinosaurs in relatively recent times.)

When you get down to details, plenty of questions come with young earth creationism. The Creation Museum and its sponsoring organization, Answers in Genesis, plan to build a multimillion-dollar full-size replica of Noah's ark. There again, questions arise. Besides the question of fitting the many created kinds inside one large boat, there's the problem of Noah's building technique. The Bible says that the ark was 300 cubits long, approximately 450 feet. By modern shipbuilding standards, this is modest: oil tankers and cruise ships can be nearly three times as long. But for wooden ships, such lengths have proven structurally problematic. How, then, did Noah do it?

Such questions might never occur to the casual reader of Genesis, but the Creation Museum cheerfully suggests answers to them. The name Answers in Genesis captures this essential focus on making sense—sense of the history of the earth and sense of human life based on the Bible.

God's Word is entirely trustworthy, the Creation Museum declares, and if we begin with its witness, we can work out the scientific details. The museum intends to instill confidence that the first chapters of Genesis are inspiringly and literally true. The Bible answers all the key questions.

———————

Georgia Purdom, who has her PhD in molecular genetics from Ohio State University, came late to young earth creationism and found her dream job at the Creation Museum. Trim and neat, with short dark hair, she is an attractive, articulate spokesperson.

Purdom, who is the same age as Todd Wood, had "a wonderful upbringing" near Columbus, Ohio. Her father was a payroll administrator for a local glass company, her mother a stay-at-home mom. They were very close. "My family was really the core. That's who I wanted to spend time with."

She was active in her Nazarene church, particularly in "Bible quizzing" where teams of students would compete against other churches regarding Bible knowledge. In her spare time she enjoyed reading Christian fiction.

Though no one in her family graduated from college, she had high ambitions. "I can never remember a time when I didn't want to be a scientist." AP biology was her favorite class at a large public high school. (They skipped the chapter on evolution.)

After her junior year of high school, she attended a summer session in environmental biology at Cedarville University, a small Baptist college in Ohio. She "fell in love with the place," especially because of its strongly Christian atmosphere. She applied to study biology there, planning to go on to medical school.

Talking to Purdom about her school experiences, one is most struck by her conscientiousness. She focused like an eagle on the grades she would need for medical school. Though Cedarville taught a six-day creation, Purdom paid the subject limited attention. She never read creationist literature. Ken Ham, the Australian schoolteacher who would later found Answers in Genesis, came to speak at the college, but she wasn't captivated. Young earth creationism remained in a distant orbit of her consciousness. It just wasn't an issue to her. Her focus was simple and practical: get good grades.

At the end of Purdom's sophomore year, a new professor came to the biology department and talked about his work in cancer research. Purdom was fascinated. She decided that she was meant for the laboratory. The next summer she did a summer internship at a hospital associated with Case Western Reserve University, working in a laboratory studying problems in immunology. "It was a great introduction to real research," she says, "and I loved it." That fall she applied to MD-PhD programs, aiming for a career in medical research.

She was dumbfounded when she didn't get in anywhere. "It was devastating. I couldn't understand." Neither could her professors. If Georgia Purdom couldn't get accepted, how could anybody?

———

The Creation Museum's main exhibit takes a visitor on a long, carefully planned route, winding through two stories of the museum. It begins with a diorama of a fossil dig. Dinosaur bones are clearly visible protruding from the ground, but two paleontologists—one a creationist, the other of a classical persuasion—disagree about the meaning of the fossilized bones. "The evidence is present. The past is interpretation" is the mantra the museum pronounces over this scene, as well as over sapphires, meteorites, trilobite tracks, and Lucy, the famous hominid fossil found in Africa. Different starting points—different assumptions—make all the difference in interpreting facts.

What starting point then? In an adjacent room the Bible, God's Word, is reverently summarized. Another display summons up the questioning of God's Word, most notably in the Scopes trial. As a visitor moves along a narrow, twisting corridor, this questioning leads to other results. "God is dead!" scream the media. We enter a ghetto environment, dark and gritty and scrawled with graffiti. The corridor widens into a dark room where videos show vignettes of societal decay: video games and Internet pornography, pregnancy and abortion, envy and gossip, and a church where a modernist preacher tells his congregation that the church must make peace with science while a teenager in the congregation fiddles with his cell phone.

Doubt the Bible, and reap the consequences. It's a dramatized version of an old-fashioned sermon on the wages of sin, though hellfire is not mentioned. Before beginning to answer questions, the Creation Museum establishes its own starting point: the Bible.

———

Purdom did not give up on science, even though graduate schools turned her down. She had a backup plan, applying for work in several university research labs. Case Western offered a position in an all-female lab led by a very positive, encouraging scientist. "She treated her lab assistants like grad students. She was a great mentor."

For most of a year Purdom dissected mice, removing nerve clusters from their spines and doing molecular analysis on them. At the same time she took a class on molecular genetics. Both experiences confirmed her interest in laboratory science, even though she experienced plenty of frustration. "Science doesn't work 90 percent of the time. Sometimes you have to work for two years to get something to work. It stinks, but that's the way it is. That's research." Purdom's determined approach to life fit well. She could be dogged in pursuing results. With the help of her mentor, she published a scientific paper on her research findings, an unusual achievement for a lab assistant.

Something else was percolating. Throughout her schooling, Purdom experienced terrible stage fright whenever she had to make a classroom speech. During her senior year in college, she was required to make a presentation for her senior seminar. Preparation was agonizing, but when Purdom's mother saw a videotape of the presentation she—always encouraging—told her she ought to be a teacher.

Teaching was not on Purdom's agenda. "I have very high standards. I knew I would be disappointed with students." During her year as a laboratory assistant, however, she thought more about her mother's comment. Life in a laboratory was very isolating. "Do I want to spend my life at a lab bench or with people?" She slowly developed "a passion to teach." Instead of applying again to medical school, she switched to PhD programs in molecular genetics. Ohio State accepted her with a fellowship. She aimed to become a college professor.

After setting its foundation in the Bible, the Creation Museum's main exhibit follows the Genesis 1–11 account. There's a majestic video of the six days of creation, followed by a bright room filled with the wonders of creation. Dioramas of the garden of Eden portray Adam's naming of the animals and the tree of life. A life-size, naked Adam and Eve meet waist-deep in a lily pond, Eve's long dark hair chastely covering her breasts.

Then comes sin. It's the same story all over again: rebel against God's command, and you reap disaster. Stark black-and-white news photos show violence and death. There's a diorama of bloody animal sacrifice—necessary to cleanse sinful humanity. Clothing is designed to cover shame. A full-size animatronic dinosaur becomes a predator, threatening human life. Snake venom, disease, death, aging—all fit into the same picture. The advent of sin quickly changed God's beautiful creation into something full of blood and death.

Previously vegetable-eating animals became scavengers to deal with a novelty: dead flesh. Cain killed his brother, Abel. Poisonous creatures, weeds—we can only speculate about how these came to be. (Did God adapt creatures already made?) Dioramas portray simple village settings where work, strife, and suffering entered human life.

Noah's flood is the next major chapter in the Creation Museum story. There's a two-story life-size model of a section of Noah's ark, suggesting just how big the original was. Then come the most science-oriented of the museum's displays, closely following the catastrophic plate tectonics theory of the Gang of Six. The Grand Canyon and Mount St. Helens are principal focal points—the canyon because geologist Stephen Austin of the Institute for Creation Research has published papers suggesting how its formation came about in the turbulent years after Noah's flood abated; Mount St. Helens because it offers an indication of dramatic changes that can occur under cataclysmic conditions.

It's piecemeal proof—there's a lot more to geology than the Grand Canyon and Mount St. Helens—but there's enough of it to make the basic point. Young earth creationists are involved with science, and they can show evidence for *their* interpretation of facts. It starts with the Bible, but it has its fingers in the world of scientific investigation.

At some places the exhibit candidly admits a lack of certainty. For example, with a mural showing how the created kinds formed diverse species since the Flood, a placard reads: "Present changes are too small and too slow to explain these differences, suggesting God provided organisms with special tools to change rapidly."

––––––––

The autumn that Purdom began graduate studies at Ohio State, her mother was diagnosed with cancer. The disease progressed very rapidly, and the end came early in the New Year. Purdom went to visit her mother every day during hospital stays. Her professors were very understanding and supportive, but the experience of watching her mother suffer was emotionally devastating.

"The cancer was very painful. In the late stages it had metastasized and spread throughout her body. It was terribly hard to see." Her mother had been her key support, praying for her, believing in her, encouraging her. When she had exams at night, her mother always called to make sure she got home safely. As her mother died, Purdom says, "I had two questions. Why death? And why me? I shook my fist at God. Why do I have to lose my mother at the age of twenty-three?"

The end came at home, with Purdom arriving too late to say a last good-bye. The next day she turned up at school as usual. People looked at her as though to say, "What are you doing here?"

"But I knew this was what my mother wanted me to do," Purdom says.

As she picked up the pieces in the following weeks and months, a group of young people at Purdom's Nazarene church in Columbus proved incredibly supportive. She met Chris Purdom there. He had never been to college. He worked in his father's steel fabrication plant, hoping to become a long-haul trucker. "I had seen many girls marry and quit [their education], and I did not want to let anything stand in my way. I had wanted to wait [to marry] until after graduate school." Some of her friends were baffled by their connection, Purdom says, since she and Chris were so different educationally. "I found that very upsetting. I don't look at a person's career. I look at their relationship to the Lord and their character." Chris was extremely supportive of her goals. They became engaged and were married a year later.

Purdom's research at Ohio State focused on the molecular genetics of bone cells and their maturation. She did well, publishing three papers. "Evolution wasn't relevant to what we did. It wasn't like we consulted Darwin's *On the Origin of Species* before work every day." She did, however, overhear discussions of creation and evolution. A court case regarding the Kansas schools' curriculum was creating controversy. One of her professors argued for evolution against one of her fellow grad students, a Christian who argued for intelligent design.

"I kept my mouth shut," Purdom says. "I knew I could get in trouble. It might be a detriment to my education."

Besides, she didn't really know what she believed. She didn't question the Genesis account, but "how do I really explain it from a scientific perspective? I began to think that I needed to know more."

She did know that she wanted to become a college professor. Looking for experience, she volunteered to teach a class in molecular genetics. "I loved it. I loved the interaction. I loved teaching and learning the material really well." She also joined an intercollegiate program intended to prepare future faculty.

After five years Purdom received her PhD. Applying only to Christian schools, she was offered a teaching position at Mount Vernon Nazarene University in Ohio. Her sister and several friends had attended there. Her husband's work in trucking didn't interfere; he could live almost anywhere. In fact, he was gone all week, so she had plenty of time to prepare for classes.

———

During her first year as a college professor, Purdom came across a familiar verse during her devotions: "Always be prepared to give an answer to everyone who asks you to give the reason for the hope that you have" (1 Peter 3:15). It arrested her attention. Remembering the grad school discussions she overheard and thinking of questions she might get at church or in class, she was troubled by her lack of clarity. She didn't know how to defend what she believed. "The Lord just hit me hard: you really need to have good answers for this."

Seeking scientific understanding, she read Michael Behe's *Darwin's Black Box.* It was her very first book on evolution from a Christian point of view, and she loved it. The detailed biological descriptions of the complexity of the cell were "just my cup of tea," confirming what she already knew: there was no way the cell could have evolved by chance. She went on to read Phillip Johnson's *Darwin on Trial.*

Intelligent Design (ID) made sense to her, as far as it went, but she was troubled by its lack of an explicit basis in Christian faith. "My goal was to lead people to Jesus Christ and to believe God's Word." ID didn't make sense of Scripture. It didn't tie things together. It didn't answer the question that troubled her most: Was the earth really millions of years old?

At the end of the school year she attended a convocation of Nazarene educators, choosing a seminar titled "The Creation-Evolution Dialogue and the Church." She was surprised by words from a professor from another Nazarene college who said that he taught evolution. He believed God set life in motion and did not otherwise intervene in the evolution of the species. "That's what I teach," he said.

One of Purdom's colleagues asked about the implication that death existed before Adam and Eve's fall, since natural selection works through culling. Humanity coming late in evolutionary history, there would have been creatures dying for millions of years before sin came into the world with Adam. "I'll never forget his answer," Purdom says. "He said, 'I have had some students question that. I just tell them, that's for the theologians to figure out. I don't deal with that.'

"It blew me away. You have to deal with it. We're all theologians. We have to know what we believe and why. That's a nonanswer."

A light went on in Purdom's head. This, she realized, was a big issue, one she had never seen whole before. Evolution portrayed millions of years of death, utterly detached from Scripture's emphasis on death coming through human sin. "That's clearly contradictory to Scripture. I knew that."

At that moment, the impact of worldviews struck her. "Initially, I am going to go look at the scientific evidence, and it's going to tell me the truth. What I began to realize is that we interpret the evidence. No scientist is truly objective. Science is, but scientists are not." In observational science such as she did in the laboratory, worldviews might make little difference. But in interpreting the past, so much depended on one's presuppositions.

If she made the Bible her presupposition, she would know that death wasn't a natural force. It was a consequence of sinful rebellion. In thinking this through, she released a powerful burden that had weighed on her since her mother's death. God was not responsible. Death was not part of his plan. Quite the contrary: by participating in spreading his gospel, she was joining God's work to undo the power of death in the world.

That summer, Purdom became a "true biblical creationist," believing in a young earth. "I read everything I could get my hands on." During school holidays she would go on her husband's cross-country truck routes, reading nonstop as he drove. Teaching an adult Sunday school class on evolution and creation forced her to learn her material well as she developed her own curriculum.

As she began to understand creationist beliefs, literature from Answers in Genesis particularly impressed her. She attended its conferences, met some of its staff, and in 2004 attended its Creation College, learning how to give effective talks to laypeople.

During the same period the mixed messages given at her university began to trouble her. It wasn't clear about young earth creationism. "I saw cracks in the institution." Purdom felt the messages were confusing students, while she "wanted so badly for people to understand this sooner than I did."

Answers in Genesis invited her to give a lunchtime lecture. Then another invitation was extended, this time with the proviso that she bring her husband along. "I thought they were interested in having me as an adjunct." Instead, they offered to make her their full-time staff scientist.

———————

Purdom is not the only scientist who works at Answers in Genesis. David Menton is a grandfatherly figure who got his PhD in biology from Brown University in the 1960s, after which he became a professor of anatomy at

Washington University School of Medicine. Retired since 2000, he offers occasional lectures at the Creation Museum, including "Three Ways to Make an Apeman."

On a Thursday afternoon his audience of about a dozen people is more than half schoolchildren. Menton treats them kindly and diverts his talk to address them directly several times. After sharing his scientific credentials, he says, "I've never seen a conflict between science and conservative Christianity." Science, he says, is what is "observable, repeatable, and testable." Evolution doesn't fit that description.

Menton's subject is the anatomy of humans and our putative human ancestors. He has brought a variety of skeletons and crania to share. Holding up skulls for examination, he explains that as an anatomist he can quite easily tell the difference between humans and apes. Humans can wear glasses, he says, because they have a protruding nose, while ape noses are flat. (Menton demonstrates glasses sliding off an ape skull.) Human faces are vertical, while those of apes slope backward. The forehead of humans is curved, with the orbit of the eye clearly visible, whereas apes have flat foreheads and their eye orbits are hidden. And finally, humans have much bigger brains.

Menton takes up the case of *Australopithecus sediba*—the fossil hominid featured in *Science* as a possible human ancestor. He gives the task of analysis over to the children present. Nose? Flat like ape. Face? Sloped like ape. Forehead and eye orbit? All ape. Brain size? Ape.

He performs the same task with *Australopithecus ramidus*, another notable recent find. This, too, is all ape.

Cro-Magnon man, however, proves to be all *Homo sapiens* by Menton's analysis. The cave people of prehistoric Europe were children of Adam. "It's simple, obvious," Menton says. Pointing out skeletal features he says, "As an anatomist, I can tell you that is a human skeleton."

In evolutionary thinking, all organisms fit on a family tree, though they may be on different branches. For young earth creationists, the proper image for life is not a tree but an orchard—many separate trees, producing different kinds of fruit. Humans are not related to other creatures—they come from different trees.

Menton's analysis is quite different from Todd Wood's, which placed *sediba* in the human category. Explaining the divergence, Wood writes, "I analyze far more variables, I do it systematically, and I try not to allow modern humans to determine what I accept as human or not. As far as I can tell, Menton looks for differences between modern humans and those fossils he *a priori* decides are apes. Otherwise, he has absolutely no way of knowing whether any of his characteristics are actually diagnostic of humans or not."

In other words, no one can be sure whether Adam had a nose that could hold up glasses. Since creation has changed dramatically since the fall (as young earth creationists believe), you can't assume that modern apes or modern humans have the same characteristics as their fossil ancestors. Wood analyzes fossils on a purely statistical basis. But Menton's more intuitive approach has the advantage that even a child can understand it.

When Purdom joined Answers in Genesis, the Creation Museum was in the construction phase. She was involved in reviewing materials for potential exhibits. When the museum opened in 2007, protesters carried signs saying, "Thou Shalt Not Lie." They didn't deter visitors from coming—three hundred thousand a year. Answers in Genesis is on the upswing as a result.

"I'm amazed at the diversity of people who come," Purdom says. "They won't go to church, but they will come here. Considering how much attention the museum gets from atheists, you know it's having an impact."

The museum contains almost no mention of genetics, Purdom's specialty. "As much as I would love to write tons on genetics and have people stand there and read it, that's not going to happen." She says the museum is dedicated to the big picture, a worldview battle.

While some outsiders are incredulous that the museum plans to build a full-size replica of Noah's ark, it makes perfect sense for Answers in Genesis. The organization wants to reach masses of people, and surveys have shown that masses are attracted to Noah's ark, just as they are to dinosaurs. A consulting firm that estimates potential audiences was "dead on" for the museum's first year at four hundred thousand. That same firm estimates one million visitors for the first year of the ark. Lacking space for parking on the current property, Answers in Genesis plans to build the ark some distance away. "It will not be an amusement park. No rides," Purdom says.

For Purdom, it's still a dream job. She gets to indulge her passion to teach, without having to grade homework. (Purdom gives talks in churches and at conferences.) She writes not only about scientific topics but also about life as a mother and wife. Regular working hours allow her time with her daughter. And she still does literature-based research, most recently on stromatolites, the algae-formed mats that (by conventional history) were some of the earliest and most abundant life on earth. Young earth creationists believe that stromatolites must have grown in special zones that were among the first to be caught in the rising floodwaters, since their fossils formed in the very lowest postflood strata. Understanding them is crucial for working out the geological boundary between pre- and postflood fossils.

Purdom attends meetings of the Creation Biology Society when she can. She is immensely encouraged by how many people are working at developing scientific understanding. "So much research needs to be done. There's an incredible amount of science that is coming out—solid, peer-reviewed science. We've really grown in that area."

Research remains a sideline for Purdom; her passion and calling is to teach. She's dubious, anyway, whether research really changes people's minds. "People want to argue evidence, but you just go around in a circle. The evidence is a confirmation of the Bible, which we already know is true."

Purdom never tires of teaching its truths. She rehearses mini-debates about evolution and the Flood with her nine-year-old daughter, who attends public school. When a teacher said dinosaurs lived millions of years ago, Purdom's daughter raised her hand to offer a contrary view.

"This is a difficult time," Purdom notes. "Kids are scientifically literate. We have to be giving them answers."

She smiles. "[Martin] Luther had his battles. This is ours."

5 Michael Behe
The Secret Cell

In Michael Behe's spartan office at Lehigh University sits a rocking chair, a gift from the school in recognition of twenty-five years teaching biochemistry. He has spent most of his professional life at the school, and the friendly, energetic Behe remains secure in his tenured position. He may be the only professor in the world, however, to have a disclaimer on a university website: "While we respect Prof. Behe's right to express his views, they are his alone and are in no way endorsed by the department. It is our collective position that intelligent design has no basis in science, has not been tested experimentally, and should not be regarded as scientific."

Behe's office is in Iacocca Hall, a large building set high on a hill overlooking the charming, historic town of Bethlehem, Pennsylvania. The building's clattering corridors are lined with doors opening on scientific laboratories. Behe, though, has no laboratory, only an office and a computer that he can use to search through scientific literature. His department took away his laboratory several years ago.

He is a short, bearded man, with the bright eyes of a hobbit. He is probably the most famous of Lehigh faculty, a man whose published works have been reviewed in *Science* and the *New York Times*. He once dreamed of doing pioneering research, exploring the vast complexities of the cell. Now lab research is out, with no prospect of renewal.

Behe does not seem bitter. He makes no complaints at all about the way he has been treated. On the other hand, he makes no effort to hide the difficulties he has been through.

————————

Behe was born on a snowy night in 1952 in Altoona, Pennsylvania, a railroad town. Both sets of grandparents lived a hardscrabble existence there, sometimes relying on bags of food from the Catholic parish. Behe's father was a local football hero—Golden Toe Behe—who reportedly holds the record for the longest field goal at the old town stadium. He served in WWII and, thanks to the GI Bill, became the first member of the family to go to college. After graduating with a degree in economics, he snagged a job with the Household Finance Corporation, which pioneered the installment loan. As a corporation man, Behe moved his growing family half a dozen times before settling down in Harrisburg. There Michael attended the St. Margaret Mary grade school and Bishop McDevitt High School.

The Behes and their eight children made up a devout family, saying the rosary most nights and attending Mass every Sunday without fail. "We read devotionals, not Aquinas," Behe says. "I was a happy-as-a-clam Catholic, sure that it was true." In high school classes, taught by nuns, he discovered his interest in science. This was never opposed to faith in the Catholic Church. Evolution, in particular, did not trouble him. "I believed in it. It was God's way of making life."

The first day of high school biology, he and his classmates were given a single-spaced sheet of definitions to memorize by Friday. He hated the class. "Too much memorization," he remembers. He did enjoy chemistry. One moment may have sealed his direction. The teacher mixed a beaker of silver nitrate solution with sodium chloride, producing a shimmering, spreading cloud. The possibility of such magical transformations drew Behe into chemistry. "I wanted to know how the world worked," he says. "Chemistry was the best bet to get me there."

He attended Drexel University in Philadelphia as a chemistry major. Drexel marked Behe's first exposure to atheists, Jews, and other non-Catholics. He grew lax in his faith, not from active disbelief, but from laziness. He stopped going to Mass.

Drexel had an unusual approach to college education: students were placed in jobs. Thus Behe worked six months of every year for a US agriculture research facility. There he learned to love biochemistry and its vast fields of the unknown. Biochemistry made him feel like the scientists who first looked through a microscope and discovered the minute complexity of the flea. "Remember, the molecular weight of [an ordinary chemical like] benzine is 78, while a protein may have a weight of 78,000. Molecules of living things are much more complex, and that attracted me."

Once he asked a professor a biochemistry question and received the reply, "That's not known yet." That appealed to Behe's vanity, he says. He wanted to pioneer the unknown, not run a laboratory for some commercial company. He decided, therefore, to go to graduate school and devote himself to academic research. He was clear about the consequences: a life of poverty. It seemed a worthy sacrifice to make.

———

For grad school, Behe moved a few blocks to the University of Pennsylvania. There he studied hemoglobin's role in sickle-cell anemia, a classic disease caused by a mutation first identified by Linus Pauling. The disease gets its name from the shape characteristically found in its victims' red blood cells. It is an incurable, painful, debilitating sickness that often leads to a premature death. Behe's research studied the effects of various dilutions of the blood's hemoglobin. "I got a problem that was pretty easy to solve but interesting. We were able to explain the behavior of these various mixtures. Everything worked."

The university awarded him a prize for his dissertation. "In one way it was good; in one way it was bad. I thought all science was going to work like this."

While happily doing science in graduate school, he began to feel that something was missing: church. When he returned to regular worship, he found it more deeply satisfying than ever before. He began to read serious Catholic authors, such as G. K. Chesterton and Dietrich von Hildebrand, and he subscribed to Catholic magazines. He even thought briefly about becoming a priest. What stopped him was his deep-seated desire to become a father.

After completing his PhD at the University of Pennsylvania, Behe went on to a postdoctorate at the National Institutes of Health (NIH) in Washington, DC. There he began work on a completely different set of questions, having to do with a newly discovered form of DNA— Z-DNA—that flips to twist left instead of the usual right. Great excitement greeted the initial find of Z-DNA. Scientists hoped that it would contribute important understanding to the way in which DNA functions in the cell. At the NIH and in subsequent faculty positions, Behe would pursue research on Z-DNA, but it would prove to be a blind alley. "Nobody could find any biological function for it. Bummer! Why doesn't nature make use of this?"

At the beginning, however, everything had promise. Behe felt that he was fulfilling his dream, probing the mysteries of life.

As he gained an increasing understanding of biochemistry, he sometimes found himself wondering about the origins of life. He once talked with his lab partner, also a Catholic, about what it would take to initiate the first cell. "You need DNA, proteins, a cell membrane. . . . 'Nah, can't happen.' We laughed and went back to work. We weren't interested in challenging orthodoxy."

He notes, however, the intellectual freedom of believers. They aren't required to believe in causal happenstance.

While working in Washington, he also dated a lab tech who was an evangelical Christian attending Fourth Presbyterian Church. He went to church services and Bible studies with her, and she attended Mass with him on occasion. For the first time in his life, he encountered religious skepticism about evolution in the person of Pastor Richard Halverson, who would later become chaplain of the US Senate. "Apples don't turn into oranges," Behe remembers Halverson saying. The critique made little headway with Behe. "Catholics don't care about evolution," he told his girlfriend, laughingly.

––––––––––

When the time came to apply for a faculty position, Behe received two offers: one from LSU in Baton Rouge, Louisiana, and one from Queens College in Queens, New York. Although he had lived in Philadelphia and in the DC metro area, Behe considered himself a country boy. He despised the idea of living in New York City. To carry on his work with Z-DNA, however, he needed an expensive piece of equipment for which LSU could not put up the money. Queens could, so he moved to New York. "To this day I consider that providential, because I met my wife."

Just before leaving Washington he subscribed to William Buckley's *National Review* magazine. There he found a personals ad inviting young Catholics to something called the New York Catholic Forum. Behe had just turned thirty. The forum featured speakers probing Catholic thought. He joined a choir that sang Latin hymns. The real reason for attending, however, appeared at a Halloween party. "A vision of loveliness came into the room, a short, raven-haired Italian girl. I finagled an introduction." It was not long before Celeste and he were engaged to be married, making plans for a large Catholic family.

Believing that New York was unsuitable for raising that family, Behe began looking for other positions. Two months after baby Grace was born, the Behes moved to Lehigh. They bought a house in the country and from the beginning homeschooled their children. That was Celeste's initiative—Behe says he thought Catholic schools would be fine. She did most of the teaching, though Behe was in charge of teaching reading when the children were small and science education in high school. (His children took little interest in pursuing science, though son Leo has recently taken up physics.) Early on the family got rid of the TV, a decision that Behe resisted, due to his love for the Philadelphia Eagles.

The Behes have nine children. Raising them has not been easy. Behe says that in the beginning Celeste would comment on other families, "I don't know why their kids act like that." Later, others applied the same comment to the Behes. Homeschool families would avoid arranging play dates. "[Raising children] was more complicated than we thought."

Nevertheless, it is evident in talking with Behe that his family is his first vocation—his heart and soul, regardless of whatever pain it has cost him. And it has, indeed, cost him pain.

———————

In 1987 the new junior faculty member at Lehigh was, to any observer, one of many thousands of laboratory scientists across America riding the wave of rapidly growing understanding of the cell. There were a few superstars in this galaxy of science—people like Francis Crick and James Watson, who discovered DNA—but most biological scientists were anonymous workers building the cathedral of knowledge a brick at a time. Behe was soon to become famous, however—or infamous, depending on your point of view.

It began when he noticed an advertisement in the Conservative Book Club for a new book, Michael Denton's *Evolution: A Theory in Crisis*. Curious, he ordered the book. "I read it in two days. I thought, *This is a great book*."

Denton, an agnostic biochemist, reviewed a wide range of evidence for evolution and found it wanting. "He was a persuasive writer, a scientist who clearly knew what he was talking about." Denton offered no alternative understanding of life; he merely pointed out problems in evolutionary theory. In reading him, Behe realized that he had never truly examined his baseline biological beliefs. Evolution was orthodoxy, and "if everybody believed it, who am I not to believe it? I didn't ask questions."

Now, though, he became a skeptic eager to share his doubts with anybody who would listen—indeed, even with those who didn't want to listen. Colleagues and grad students bore the brunt of his enthusiasm. (His wife, a good Catholic, continued not to care about evolution.) Looking back, Behe can view this phase with humor. "You have this wide-eyed guy coming up to you and saying, 'It's a lie!'"

He got very little response—mostly smiles. "I began to feel triumphalistic, as though I was smarter than other folks. It was clear to me that they didn't have answers to Denton's questions, in fact didn't even know there was an issue. It made me feel unique."

One part of Denton's critique Behe knew best: the cell. The exploding knowledge that he and other scientists were gaining revealed an astonishingly complex machine—complex enough to make a watch seem downright simple. How could such a thing come into being through just the chance collision of molecules? "I looked for explanations or partial explanations in the journals and found nothing. I found [genome] sequence comparisons only. I wanted to know mechanisms."

"Ninety percent or more of evolutionary articles are on common descent." But Behe was untroubled by common descent. Parallel genetic sequences in different organisms didn't answer his questions. He knew that organisms had basic similarities. What he wanted to know was how those similarities had been built. "I'm thinking blood clotting, the bacterial flagellum," and other intricate mechanisms of the cell. "Nobody studied how they came to be. Nobody offered a pathway of how they came to be built up. Nobody seemed even interested."

For all his fervor, Behe soon reached a dead end. He could talk, but nobody really listened. He wrote one op-ed piece for the local paper expressing his doubts and suggesting that Darwinism had problems. But the article didn't generate any discussion. He was busy generating scientific papers and grants, trying to get tenure. The subject lay fallow until, in 1991, Phillip Johnson published his book *Darwin on Trial*.

––––––––

In the fall of 1987, Johnson was a middle-aged law professor at the University of California, Berkeley, taking a sabbatical year in England. His distinguished academic career had specialized in criminal law and lately branched out into more philosophical fields of legal theory. Nevertheless, Johnson could not shake the feeling that his life amounted to a wasted talent, that he had used a first-class mind for only second-class occupations. He was "looking for something to do with the rest of his life" and talked about it with his wife, Kathie, as they hiked around the green fields of England. "I pray for an insight," he told her. "I'd like to have an insight that is worthwhile and not just be an academic who writes papers and spins words."

In London, Johnson's daily path from the bus stop to his office at University College took him by a scientific bookstore. "Like a lot of people," Johnson says, "I couldn't go by a bookstore without going in and fondling a few things." The very first time he walked by he saw and purchased the powerful, uncompromising argument for Darwinian evolution by Richard Dawkins, *The Blind Watchmaker*. Johnson devoured it and then Denton's *Evolution: A Theory in Crisis*. "I read these books, and

I guess almost immediately I thought, *This is it. This is where it all comes down to, the understanding of creation."*

Johnson began a furious reading program, absorbing the literature on Darwinian evolution. Within a few weeks he told his wife, "I think I understand this stuff. I know what the problem is. But fortunately, I'm too smart to take it up professionally. I'd be ridiculed. Nobody would believe me. They would say, 'You're not a scientist. You're a law professor.' It would be something, once you got started with it, you'd be involved in a lifelong, never-ending battle."

"That," says Johnson, remembering with a smile, "was of course irresistible. I started to work the next day."

Johnson grew up as a brainy wunderkind in the town of Aurora, Illinois. Nicknamed "Red" for his red hair, he was proud of his reputation for fighting. By his own recollections, he was arrogant and obnoxious, too smart for his own good. Reading the Harvard University catalog, he discovered that on rare occasions the school considered applications from high school juniors. He applied and was accepted. He could hardly wait to get out of town.

After four years at Harvard he went on to law school at the University of Chicago. There, finally, he discovered a course of study to challenge him. After graduation he clerked for the chief justice of the California Supreme Court and for Earl Warren, chief justice of the United States Supreme Court. He went on to teach at Berkeley.

Berkeley was an ideal platform for a brilliant legal scholar. Its charged atmosphere worked to shake Johnson free from conventional thinking, especially during the turbulent 1960s and 1970s. Johnson despised the groupthink he saw on the Left, but perversely, he found himself envying the radicals. "Misguided as they were, they believed in something, and I was just doing my institutional duty. That whole experience led me to begin to ask, what is so great about this agnostic rationalism I have been taught?"

He and his wife had agreed to divorce. One day before they broke the news to their children, Johnson went to a place he very rarely encountered: a church. His eleven-year-old daughter was attending vacation Bible school at the invitation of a neighbor. She wanted a parent to attend the final dinner, and Johnson said he would go. Understandably, he had a lot on his mind as he listened to the pastor make a brief presentation.

"To this day I can't remember any of the content of it. What I remember thinking at the time was, *You know, he really believes this—and I could too. I could be like that.* It became part of my plausibility structure. Why not? What's so good about what I've got?"

At some friends' invitation, he began attending First Presbyterian Church of Berkeley and eventually made a Christian commitment. He met Kathie, another adult convert, at the church. The scene was set for his life-changing decision to embrace the role of revolutionary in science.

He did not look like a revolutionary. His red hair was gone, and he carried a large, round, spectacled head on his body as one might balance a pumpkin. Not only did he look innocuous, but he also acted it: friendly and gregarious to adversaries as much as to friends. Underneath the bland exterior, however, Phillip Johnson remained a fighter.

Given Michael Behe's skepticism about evolution, he was bound to read *Darwin on Trial*, the book that eventually came from Johnson's English sabbatical. Behe appreciated the book's logical appeal, though it did not address the scientific issues that concerned him. Johnson claimed that the scientific establishment was repressing questions about evolution. Repression was not exactly what Behe had experienced thus far, but he did think evolution deserved more scrutiny.

When *Science* published an article about *Darwin on Trial*, Behe was annoyed at its dismissive tone. Uncharacteristically, he wrote a letter to the magazine, which its editors published. His message had to do with how scientists responded to nonscientists: "This guy is smart. He's a layman with questions. Instead of waving him off, why don't you engage him on the topic?"

Johnson read Behe's letter and recognized the power of a defender from within the science establishment. Immediately, he wrote. Behe was flattered to receive a friendly letter from a published author. Johnson encouraged him to write a similar letter to *Nature*, the British science magazine. (Behe did, but the letter was never published.)

Behe did not immediately grasp the significance of this interaction: "I got into Phillip Johnson's mind." Even before *Darwin on Trial* was published, Johnson had become the leader of a small loose-knit group that would become the core of the Intelligent Design (ID) movement. A lucid proponent of the ID point of view, a keen battle strategist, and a formidable intellectual presence, Johnson understood that he could change nothing unless he had allies. He wanted to enlist Behe.

Six months after his letter to *Science* appeared, Behe received a telephone call from a Texan named Jon Buell. His Foundation for Thought and Ethics had published *Of Pandas and People*, an illustrated book questioning evolution and suggesting that an intelligent agent must be behind the origin of new organisms. Buell invited Behe to take part in an event honoring Phillip Johnson's book. Behe's first reaction was negative. He thought the "event" would probably take place in a church basement, replete with Bible-thumpers and yellers. "I didn't want to do that."

When Buell said he was inviting philosopher Michael Ruse, however, Behe switched tracks. Ruse was a prominent figure in debates about science. The event was not going to take place in a church basement. Pressed to make a commitment on the spot, Behe agreed to go to Texas.

In a daytime session on the campus of Southern Methodist University, Behe was paired with a biochemist from Texas Tech. About one hundred people attended, including biochemistry grad students. It was Behe's first time ever in such a spotlight, and he was excited. He had prepared meticulously for his talk about the formation of proteins, but his dialogue partner from Texas Tech did not seem to have done the same. Afterward, the conference organizers gave Behe encouraging slaps on the back, and Johnson said he wished Behe had a bigger audience. "I gained confidence. I had arguments [against evolution] that nobody there could answer. After that, I was anxious to debate other folks."

Not only had he gained confidence; he had gained a new set of friends. "I liked them all. We were a secret cell. Nobody knew about us, but we had plans."

Johnson invited Behe to a meeting at Pajaro Dunes, on the coast of California. "I had never been to California. I thought it was cool as heck." At the meeting were all the key players in the emerging ID movement: Paul Nelson, Jonathan Wells, William Dembski, and Stephen Meyer, among others. They met together for presentations and discussions, with plenty of free time for private conversations. Here Behe first presented the idea of *irreducible complexity*.

Simply put, the argument is that any complex machine—a mousetrap, for example—has multiple parts, none of which has function on its own. It is irreducibly complex because removing any part will cause the whole machine to cease functioning. Such machines, Behe asserted, cannot be explained by evolution because all the parts must come together at once in order for it to have any useful function. A mousetrap cannot evolve by chance; there must be a design ordering its assembly. Even more the cell. Behe's work in biochemistry made him intensely aware of just how complicated the assembly of life would be.

Everyone at the meeting seemed impressed by the new argument. Behe's confidence grew.

Besides the excitement of advancing a new idea in the "secret cell," Behe had a further reason to explore new horizons. The long decline of his research into Z-DNA was reaching its culmination, and it wasn't panning out. Behe was far from certain what further options he could pursue in his scientific research.

In his excitement, he had forgotten to pack a toothbrush. He approached Johnson and asked him where he could buy one. Ever friendly, Johnson offered to drive him to a store. Along the way, Behe summoned courage and asked, "How do you get a book published?" Johnson answered with "immortal advice: 'Get an agent.'"

Others at the meeting offered publishing contacts. Behe was advised to write four chapters and send them to an agent. "I was psyched about writing a book." Returning to Bethlehem, he pounded out four chapters explaining biochemical techniques. "I don't think any of them made it into the book." Nevertheless, publishers were interested; the sense of impending controversy attracted them. One day Behe received an e-mail informing him that the Free Press had offered a fifty-thousand dollar advance if he would say yes that afternoon.

The actual writing took a year and six months, with repeated, depressingly heavy revisions from his editors at Free Press. Nevertheless the day came, in the summer of 1996, when he stood on a beach in Ocean City, Maryland, admiring the cover of a book with his name on it. *Darwin's Black Box* was in print.

To that point, Behe had experienced no real controversy. He wrote his faculty colleagues about *Darwin's Black Box* six months before publication. He made copies of the proofs and left them in the department office for anyone to read. His chair was impressed by his attempt at openness, Behe says. Only one colleague came to talk; most people ignored the matter.

The reviews poured in: the *New York Times*, the *Wall Street Journal*, *Nature*, *National Review*. Every publication Behe cared about featured his book. "I was reviewed by *Aboard*, the magazine for the Bolivian National Airlines—a four-page review." The book was translated into a dozen languages. When the Chinese edition arrived, Behe's brother Joe said, "Now you know how I feel when I read your book."

Reviews were frequently critical, sometimes extremely so. Behe was surprised. He honestly expected people to read and to be convinced. He tried to defend himself in every publication, writing letters in response to the criticisms.

He began to receive invitations for speaking engagements. "I thought it was great. I was happy to spread the word." He expected that speaking would allow him to explain in more detail, which would surely win his adversaries over. In practice, however, it was not so simple. He remained very confident in his presentation—it seemed to him that critics missed the point much of the time—but his listeners seemed to be on a different wavelength. "The debate was quickly cast as another Scopes trial, with scientists battling fundamentalists. You can imagine I was very surprised since I'm a Catholic." Behe found that he had accidentally wandered into an ancient dispute. "I had never heard of the 'God of the gaps' before."

Still, the publicity was more good than bad. In September, Pope John Paul II issued a statement on evolution, and the *New York Times* asked Behe to respond. His op-ed drew more attention to his book. Lehigh's vice president for development, glad to see the university represented in such a prestigious publication, wrote a letter of appreciation to Behe.

He experienced no hostility from his colleagues. "Some in the chemistry department were enthusiastic. In the biology department, not so much." Looking back on that time, he describes his work as "a curiosity." Colleagues asked him what it was like to be reviewed in the *New York Times.* "There was no hostility or fear. That would not come until five or six years later."

———

Gradually, the climate grew hotter. Behe thinks the Internet played a role. "The Intelligent Design movement and the Internet grew together."

He began to get hostile e-mails out of nowhere, and so did his department chair. The curiosity that had greeted intelligent design faded, to be replaced by the sense that it posed a threat to science.

The ID movement embraced Johnson's *wedge strategy*, which argued that the theory of evolution represented a purely materialistic philosophy, much as atheists like Richard Dawkins (*The Blind Watchmaker*) said it did. By setting the rules of investigation such that God could not be invoked, evolutionary scientists had limited their "god" to the power of blind chance. Evolution was thus not science so much as atheism from the ground up. It was the perfect expression of materialistic philosophy.

One result of this focus was that ID proponents spent more energy on philosophical arguments than they did on the actual scientific evidence for or against evolution. What might have been an academic or scientific discussion became part of the culture wars—atheists on one side and believers on the other. Johnson refused to distinguish ID from young earth creationism, even though most, if not all, ID adherents believed in a millions-year-old earth; and Behe accepted common descent, the belief that all living creatures are part of a single family tree. Johnson thought believers should submerge their differences in order to battle a common enemy, atheistic science.

As a movement ID began to pay attention to public schools, urging them to "teach the controversy" by including evidence against evolution in their science classes and allowing teachers to present both ID and evolution in their classrooms. Controversial and widely publicized court cases followed, capped by the court case known simply as *Dover*.

Behe says he knew very little about the way ID was being pursued. He wasn't part of strategic or philosophical discussions; his interest was in the science, where he continued to contend for his point of view.

He received a phone call from a lawyer at the Thomas More Law Center, asking whether he would serve as an expert witness to explain ID for a trial pitting the ACLU versus the Dover, Pennsylvania, school board.

Behe had the impression that it would require perhaps half an hour on the witness stand. Innocently, he agreed.

Thomas More Law Center is well known among social conservatives for its legal activism. The center had offered legal support for the Dover, Pennsylvania, school board in its decision to require biology teachers to mention evidences against evolution and to refer students to the book *Of Pandas and People*, copies of which had been donated to the school. Sued by the ACLU on behalf of Dover parents in December 2004, the school board called on Thomas More for legal defense.

Behe was to learn later that the Discovery Institute, which had become the institutional embodiment of ID, did not support the *Dover* case. The organization urged the school board to drop the mandatory teaching of ID and not to go to court defending the right to use it in the school's curriculum. At the time he agreed to testify, Behe knew nothing about this, he says.

As Behe tells the story, *Dover* drew him in unwittingly. First, in addition to his testimony, Thomas More lawyers asked for a written statement explaining ID. He produced a twenty-page document. Next he was asked to write a rebuttal to the testimony of a paleontologist. Then he was deposed for eight hours, facing a barrage of questions. "It was not pleasant, though I was happy with how I did. I'm *still* happy with how I did. When I read the news reports, I would wonder what parallel universe these people were in."

Behe's contributions continued to grow, as he was asked to go over testimony with lawyers as they prepared for court. Ken Miller, a professor at Brown University whom Behe had debated several times, served as a lead witness for the opposition. Miller's persuasive presentation worried the Thomas More lawyers, and they fretted with Behe over how to respond.

The case dragged on for weeks before Behe was given his day in court. Actually, he had three entire days of testimony. He had never been in court before, and he found it a remarkable experience. "You learn it often matters not a whit what you say." He talked and answered questions for six hours each day, but very little of what he said made it into the judge's final opinion and even less into news accounts. For example, he pointed out that the big bang might have religious implications, but nobody barred it from science classes. "That did not make it into the judge's opinion," he notes.

What did make news was his contention under questioning that astrology was science. He meant to speak historically, for indeed, astrology and astronomy grew from the same root in the Middle Ages, and at one stage it would have been difficult to say which was science and which was not. But Behe's comment inadvertently cast him in the stereotype of a religious believer who is willing to grant irrational beliefs the status of science.

After his testimony ended, a knot of reporters greeted Behe at the courthouse door. From the way they spoke to him, he got a very positive impression of how he had done. "Reading the judge's opinion, though, I realized I was not so persuasive." The judge issued a strong judgment disallowing ID from classroom presentations, on the grounds that it was religion, not science. To a great extent the judge copied the ACLU's summaries of the evidence, Behe says. "I think he was out of his depth." More significantly, "a courtroom is not a place to settle academic disputes. I could have been Demosthenes and not made an impression."

Dover proved to be a watershed, especially at Lehigh. The chair of the biology department received many e-mails complaining about Behe: "Is Lehigh turning into a Bible college?" Some of Lehigh's graduate students were harassed when they went for employment interviews.

The university felt obliged to respond to "this evolution question," initiating a series of lectures on evolution, bringing Behe's antagonist Miller and science education activist Eugenie Scott to campus. "I thought it was great," Behe says. "They were legitimate guys."

It was at this time that the disclaimer went up on the website.

Despite all this unfavorable attention, Behe claims to feel completely comfortable at Lehigh. "I don't begrudge them their opinions. Deep down there's some resentment in me, but I never let it surface. We get along extremely well. I'm not a target."

The controversy had nothing to do with his losing laboratory space, Behe says. The reality was that his research grants had run out, and he had failed in his attempts to renew them. Research in Z-DNA was dead, and funding agencies showed no interest in his new interest in ID. He didn't have any grad students. He had to give way to other scientists who could use the space.

Behe's isolation at Lehigh has undoubtedly been painful, but less so than an unfolding drama at home. His son Leo started college at Lehigh, where he got free tuition, but shortly left school and disappeared. After a time he returned home, but over the next two years showed no interest in school or job.

Then Behe's brother Joe sent him an e-mail, urging that he look at an Internet link. Leo had posted on a blog site identifying himself as Behe's son and declaring himself an atheist. News spread quickly; soon a lengthy, illustrated interview with Leo appeared in the *Humanist*, describing his journey away from faith (persuaded by reading Richard Dawkins's *The God Delusion*) and his family's reaction. He spoke appreciatively, if a trifle condescendingly, of his father.

As ever, Behe is philosophical. He notes that as an atheist, Leo became "a nicer fellow" and "an enthusiastic student" of philosophy at nearby East Stroudsburg University. Leo recently transferred to Lehigh to study physics.

It has nevertheless been a delicate balancing act, living with Leo in his state of public unbelief. When he wanted to share his beliefs with his younger siblings, his mother told him to either shut up or move out. Behe warned him not to mention the family in his blog posts. "I won't have a reporter living in my home."

When Behe published *Darwin's Black Box*, he felt that it summed up all he had to say on the subject, now and forever. Twenty years of controversy have not changed his views. Preparing a new anniversary edition, he found that the only changes he would make would be to add his three youngest children's names to the acknowledgments.

Darwin's Black Box is essentially a simple argument. What makes it unusual (and not so simple to read) is its detailed description of cellular systems. The structures of the cell are overwhelmingly, elegantly complex. It takes Behe considerable detailed description to convey that. His point is basic, however: these things don't just happen by chance. Behe updated the centuries-old watchmaker argument: if you find a stone, you can't be sure of its cause. But if you find a watch, you readily intuit a watchmaker, whatever the process of its manufacture. Behe tried to make this argument logically watertight (thus irreducibly complex) and to apply it to the cell, the "watch" found by modern biology.

Behe got huge satisfaction from *Darwin's Black Box*. In the years after writing it, he kept wondering how he could build on the argument. The book was fundamentally an exercise in logic, not science. It is very difficult to prove a negative—that random variation and selection can never produce complex parts of the cell—and your best shot is probably logic, not science. What would you test for to confirm that nothing new could happen? Nevertheless, Behe looked for experimental evidence to confirm his point. In order to see what evolution could and could not do, he wanted huge populations of organisms undergoing rapid multiplication. He found it in the malarial parasite.

The Edge of Evolution was published in 2007, eleven years after *Darwin's Black Box*. It attempts to estimate the kinds of change that Darwinian evolution—which Behe accepts as real—can effect and find the "edge" beyond which unguided evolution cannot go. In using malaria for his centerpiece, Behe harked back to his graduate school research on hemoglobin, which malaria targets. Malarial parasites clearly evolve in response to antimalarial drugs, and biochemists have untangled some of the necessary genetic changes. Behe concludes that when a single mutation is required, malarial parasites develop drug resistance very quickly; when two separate mutations are needed, as is the case for the drug chloroquine, resistance develops much more slowly. It does develop, Behe claims, but only because of the vast numbers of malarial organisms involved. For organisms with fewer numbers and slower reproduction—mammals, for example—a double mutation would be extraordinarily unlikely. And the vastly more complicated mutations necessary for a new structure to develop would be all but mathematically impossible. Thus the edge of evolution is for very limited change.

Edge enjoyed no grace period. Scientists immediately and heartily attacked it in reviews in such publications as *Nature*, *Science*, and the *New York Times*. Those critiques often focused on Behe's statistical and genetic understanding, which biological scientists found deficient. They insisted that complex cellular parts like the bacterial flagellum were built up in a step-by-step process where different parts were borrowed or adapted from other uses.

Less commented on were later sections of the book where, answering his critics, Behe reveals that his argument still has more to do with philosophy than science. He is not really arguing for or against any particular mechanism by which the mechanisms of the cell were made. His point is that life was planned.

"Suppose you have a bacteria that doesn't have a flagellum, floating along some pond. All of a sudden from different regions of the sky UV light comes and hits the [bacterial] DNA and produces a thousand mutations that all together confer upon it a flagellum. If you could somehow trace each of those rays of light back in history, you would see that each of them arose ultimately in the big bang."

Behe doesn't mean this example literally. He uses it to make the point that you don't necessarily have to have God sticking his finger into the picture in order to create a bacterial flagellum. It could happen by the confluence of multiple mutations. However, those mutations could never occur at once unless extraordinary conditions occur.

And it could be that extraordinary conditions existed to create fully elaborated life from the time of the big bang. Behe notes that biologists like Ken Miller and Francis Collins, Christians who oppose his ideas about intelligent design, willingly embrace the so-called anthropic principle—the idea of a universe fine-tuned for life in its physical constants. Physicists have noted dozens of physical constants—everything from the strength of gravity to the density of frozen water—that must be precisely as they are, without the tiniest variation, for life as we know it to happen on planet Earth. Behe extends the idea of fine-tuning into biology. "Fine-tuning is all of a piece. It doesn't stop before life; it extends into life."

Not that Behe is committed to the idea of a universe fine-tuned for life from the beginning. "Maybe there was guidance along the way. I don't think we have enough evidence to decide between the two. But [we have] plenty of evidence to assert that things were designed, because the design is visible in the present system itself, just like it's visible in the mousetrap."

Behe's concern is not evolution, for he accepts that all life is related and that organisms developed gradually one from another. His concern is what he calls Darwinism, which he identifies with unplanned, unguided development. "Darwin's claim to fame was that [evolution] needed no teleology, no guidance, just like the wind blowing here and there filtered by natural selection. . . . That's the heart of Darwinism, and the only interesting part, as far as I am concerned."

Asked what difference ID would make to the scientist in his laboratory, Behe acknowledges its very limited significance. But it's the same with Darwinism, he says. Scientists work to figure out how things work, and the framework that they use—whether Darwinism or intelligent design—has little impact on their experiments.

———

The curiosity and excitement that characterized the early days of the intelligent design "secret society" are gone. Instead, ID has become an ideological litmus test. Behe remembers a call-in TV talk show where a caller told him, "Admit to me, you're another evangelical wanting to get conservatives on the Supreme Court."

"Most biologists haven't read my book, including most members of my department," Behe says. "It's become so controversial, it's hard to approach with a fresh mind."

Nevertheless, Behe is upbeat. "I'm very optimistic ID will prevail, not because of anything I have done, but because that's where the data are going. Biology is getting more complex, not less, to levels we didn't even know about when I wrote *Darwin's Black Box.* Darwinism is toast, clearly."

Whereas scientists reviewing Behe's book insist that his ideas have been massively disproved—and it is true that he has won no support among other biologists—Behe sees nothing in their arguments. "There's a cottage industry producing papers refuting design." To his eye, it's the old story of the "Emperor's New Clothes." "It's not that the kid is so smart," Behe says of his role. "But the data will out. Every major discovery [in biochemistry] has shown more and more complexity, and that's not favorable to Darwinism."

Meanwhile he carries on teaching two classes a semester and reading scientific journals, looking for connections, trolling for ideas. "I don't think I could spend my time more productively than reviewing the literature. Oftentimes new ideas come from outside the field, where they are not constrained by old paradigms." He admits that he misses laboratory science. "A large part of my image was in being a lab scientist.

"I have my friends. I have my family. I'm really cool in homeschool circles." It's a melancholy outcome for a scientist who dreamed of great discoveries, but Behe maintains serenity. Now in his sixties, he is playing for history.

6 Fazale Rana
Found by a Designing God

It is highly ironic that Fazale Rana meets the American public through his foreign-sounding name because nobody could be more classically American. Growing up in West Virginia, he always dreaded the first day of school when a new teacher would call his name and inevitably mispronounce it. Though raised a Muslim by his Punjabi-immigrant physics professor father, Rana saw himself as that All-American classic, the rebel. He looked and sounded 100 percent American because he was.

His rebellion was innocent stuff, dedicated to annoying teachers and making his peers laugh. Rana got As without studying. He was the best student in his high school, though the administration wouldn't let him join the National Honors Society because of his shockingly irreverent behavior. "Sports, girls, and rock and roll" were his theme, and he loved to drive the hills of West Virginia with his friends, looking for trouble.

Such youthful indulgences began to change in college when he couldn't quite cruise through his classes anymore. Studying seriously, he fell in love with biology. "I was literally entering into another world—so elegant, so fascinating. I was fascinated by how life works at the molecular level." He was drawn equally to the deeper questions it raised—"Where did life come from?" and even "What is life?"

Rana says biochemistry appeals to renegades and mavericks, people who follow unusual avocations outside their labs. "They tend to be the bad boys of science, and that attracted me."

After graduating from West Virginia State University, Rana began a PhD in biochemistry at Ohio University. No grad student has ever been more enthusiastic. He dove into research and before his first term was up had done work that would lead to two published papers. Rana wanted to learn everything. He quizzed fellow grad students about what they were learning through their research. He read chapters that were not assigned. One of his biochemistry texts had several chapters on abiogenesis— research into the origins of life. Rana learned of models proposing to explain how the first organic life began in a chemical soup of primeval earth. And he thought, *It doesn't add up.*

"In my research I was working with these phospholipids, which are pretty simple molecules. We were trying to purify these phospholipids from egg yolks, then cleave off part of the molecule and attach a synthetic component that you could monitor with instruments. It's relatively simple biochemistry, but to get those experiments to work was unbelievably difficult."

In the precise environment of the laboratory, highly skilled experimentalists struggled to manipulate molecules into new configurations. He couldn't imagine how the elegant and extraordinary machinery of the cell could self-assemble in the chaotic environment of the planet. "I could see how a protein could come into existence that might actually have function. Or how you might generate lipids occasionally." But even the simplest cell imaginable was an extraordinary factory of precisely moving parts. It could never "just happen."

There has got to be a mind, he thought. *I don't know who or what the mind is, but somebody had to start life.*

These thoughts led nowhere, however. "One thing that's unfortunate about science education," Rana says, "is that scientists are extremely well trained but poorly educated." They are trained in a scientific method that doesn't invoke God, and they know nothing of other sources of knowledge such as philosophy or religion. In fact, had Rana told his adviser that he wanted to take a course in the philosophy of science, he would have been considered nutty. Philosophy was "for people who can't do science."

Nor could Rana turn to a religious tradition. His father, a devout but very private Muslim, had raised his sons to adopt a Muslim identity. Rana's mother was Catholic, though she rarely attended Mass. Neither religion meant anything to Rana. During his sophomore year of high school he had tried out his father's faith, devoting himself to learning Islamic prayers and to reading the Koran in translation. But he found the Koran impenetrable and the prayers mystifying; he abandoned the effort.

He toyed with Universalism. Perhaps the Mind who made life revealed himself to all the religions of the world. These were mainly idle thoughts, however. Rana had no idea how to follow them up.

———————

To the extent that he thought about religious issues, Rana was agnostic. His fiancée, Amy, was a nominal Christian whose childhood faith had drifted away. They never talked about such issues. They met early on in college, studied chemistry and biology together, and planned to be married the summer after she graduated. Then she would join Rana in graduate school, both of them pursuing PhDs. Science was their common starting point, and religion was utterly irrelevant.

Until Easter, that is, when a woman who rented a room from Amy's mother invited Amy and her mother to attend church. The experience of that small pentecostal assembly penetrated Amy. There on the spot, without any preparation, she rededicated her life to God.

When Amy called Rana to tell him what happened, she introduced something startlingly new, a kind of conversation they never had before. Rana never considered sharing his thoughts with Amy while musing about the origins of life, for example. It wasn't his style to talk about such things. Now he drew the line clearly. It was fine for her if she wanted to involve herself with religion, but as for him, he was a scientist.

He didn't feel he was close-minded. During college he had occasionally gone with African American friends to their pentecostal churches. (West Virginia State is a historically black institution.) Another friend, the son of a Baptist pastor, sometimes discussed young earth creationism with him. None of these experiences led him to take Christians very seriously.

Having set his limits, Rana thought he was finished with the subject. He did not recognize Amy's increasing concern. Her new pastor mentioned the concept of being unequally yoked, the apostle Paul's warning in 2 Corinthians 6:14 that Christians should not form partnerships with non-Christians. The pastor's words weren't aimed at her, but Amy took them to heart. She wanted to do what was right, and this Bible verse seemed clear: she couldn't marry Rana if he didn't share her faith. The wedding was approaching—August 9. She began asking members of the church to pray. Very quickly, her concern spread through the entire body.

But she didn't tell Rana. Instead, Amy told him that they needed to meet with the pastor to talk about details of the wedding. Rana resisted. He didn't want to meet with Pastor Johnny, whom he thought would probably pester him about God. Amy was adamant, however. She said the pastor wouldn't marry them if they didn't meet.

So Rana reluctantly drove the hour and a half to Charleston, West Virginia, to meet with Pastor Johnny. As it turned out, the experience was not unpleasant. Johnny wasn't overaggressive in his appeal. He talked about his own faith and how much he loved reading the Bible. He appealed to Rana's pride as a scientist, suggesting that he shouldn't just dismiss something he hadn't even read.

Rana had to admit he had a point. He purchased the cheapest edition of a King James Bible he could find and began reading it in the lab after the day's work was done. At first he skipped around, unsatisfyingly. Amy suggested that he try the gospel of John. Somehow he got confused and read Matthew instead.

He was pleased to find the Christmas story there, which he vaguely knew. He went on to the Sermon on the Mount. Alone at his bench in the deserted laboratory, he encountered something strange and fearful. It was as though he could hear Jesus himself speaking the words. He felt in the core of his being that these words were true and that he could not possibly live up to them.

In his state of alarm and confusion, Rana remembered that someone had given him a pamphlet describing how to become a Christian. Now he was urgently interested. He found the pamphlet and leafed through it, absorbing these new and compelling ideas. There by himself, following the directions in the booklet, he prayed to God and committed himself to follow him.

From that day, Rana began absorbing Christianity with the same intensity he brought to biochemistry. Every weekend he drove to Pastor Johnny's church to join Amy in worship.

With Pastor Johnny's encouragement, he told his parents what he had done. His mother wept, crying that he had joined a cult. His father was furiously agitated and threatened to disown him. He baited Rana with distorted versions of the Bible's message, knowing that Rana had little knowledge of what the Bible really taught. Rana's father was a strict disciplinarian, a principled and unbending man who expected the highest standards from his sons. He felt that his son's conversion made him a failure as a father, that it represented a judgment on him. He couldn't get past it. After a number of shouting arguments, a grudging silence fell over the father-son relationship.

———————

By the best index of success in science, Rana did very well, publishing ten scientific papers on the way to concluding his doctorate. In the process he learned that while he was not outstanding in the laboratory (Amy was much more adept), he was good at seeing connections between different specializations, taking insights or techniques from one area into another and achieving results. Rana went on to do postdoctorates at the University of Virginia and at the University of Georgia, where he published six more papers. He set his sights on a career in academic research. (Amy, meanwhile, stopped her education with a master's degree; the pressures of raising children while she and her husband were studying were too great.)

He and Amy joined a series of strong and lively churches. In Athens, Ohio, a Christian who started a homeless shelter in his basement mentored Rana. Concern for the poor thus came to him as a foundation of Christian faith. He was stimulated by good teaching and excited by his involvement in fellowship and ministry. As the years went by, he wondered whether he should give up science in order to devote himself to ministry.

He felt no direct conflict between the two realms, but he didn't experience many connections either. "Nor was I looking for connections. I was never secretive about my faith, but I didn't go out of my way to tell people in the laboratory about it." His life was neatly and comfortably compartmentalized. He was satisfied with his life as a Christian and satisfied with his life as a scientist. The two did not much intersect.

———————

Rana's postdoctoral year at the University of Georgia went particularly well. His research proceeded successfully, and he and Amy liked their church immensely. His adviser and mentor was applying for a substantial NIH grant that might enable Rana to get a long-term job instead of existing on a meager postdoctoral salary.

One day his mentor grabbed him and said he had signed him up to do an interview with Procter and Gamble, the consumer products manufacturer. "I'm not trying to get rid of you, but I need you to interview because nobody has signed up and we want to keep them coming. We put you down for eleven o'clock."

Rana hustled to put together an updated CV and then showed up for the interview in jeans and a holey T-shirt. He teased the interviewer that Procter and Gamble owed him a job; he had two kids in diapers and bought unthinkable quantities of P&G's Pampers. Rana didn't take the interview seriously, but he was the only interviewee who was offered an on-site visit.

It was a free trip to Cincinnati, and he was curious to see the kind of research that the company was talking about. He presented his research in a seminar for company scientists, then went on a tour of company headquarters. Procter and Gamble surprised him with its well-equipped laboratories and serious scientific research. When he was offered an "obscene" amount of money, he realized he needed to think about it.

His mentor had been turned down for his NIH grant, apparently for political reasons. Rana had no secure future, and Amy was pregnant with their third child. *This may not be my first choice, but I need to do the responsible thing*, Rana thought. He took the job.

In Cincinnati, Amy began teaching biology at a local community college. She had an idea: What if she taught evolution by assigning her students a paper comparing it to young earth creationism? She had no interest in young earth creationism but thought that the controversy might spark student interest. At a local Christian bookstore she bought a variety of creationist literature and put it on reserve at the college library. When the term was over, she brought those books home.

Curious, Rana picked up the books. He had never given creationism a thought. When he read what Amy brought home, he was mortified. "They were just horrible science." In areas he was deeply familiar with, such as the chemistry of radiometric dating, or entropy and the second law of thermodynamics in biological systems, the authors appeared not to understand the subject. "I could understand why there was resistance to the Christian faith on the part of scientists if this is how people are arguing."

The books served one purpose, though: they stimulated Rana's curiosity. He began to read everything he could find on evolution. He read Stephen Jay Gould, Stuart Kauffman, and Michael Denton, scientists who questioned evolutionary dogma from purely nonreligious perspectives. "Here was skepticism about evolution that seemed to be scientifically robust."

In all his education, he had never really studied evolution in depth. He had assumed that if he went deeper into evolutionary theory, the evidence for it would become stronger. That had been the case in biochemistry as he went from a superficial to a deeper understanding. Now he began to wonder whether studying evolution would yield the same kind of depth.

Then he happened on *Creator and the Cosmos*, a book by astronomer Hugh Ross, an evangelical Christian. The book said very little about biology, focusing on astronomy and physics, fields where Rana knew very little. What attracted him was Ross's attitude. He seemed to take science and Scripture with equal seriousness, bringing them together. He wrote about the big bang and its correspondence to Genesis 1:1. He described the fine-tuning of the universe necessary for life to emerge. Rana looked up the references and found that they were accurate: the scientific literature said exactly what Ross said it did. Ross made a case, through science, that the creator God really did exist.

"I was fascinated that Ross didn't believe in evolution either." He tried to think what things would look like if evolution were true. To his mind, the fossil record didn't fit. It showed sudden explosions of new life-forms and then long periods of stasis. That, he reflected, is what you would expect if the Creator were intervening, making new creatures.

Previously, he had toyed with theistic evolution, a position in which God remained hands-off as evolution ran its course. He had alarmed his wife by speculating over whether Adam and Eve were real historical persons. Now, however, he began to adopt Hugh Ross's ideas of progressive creation. Ross believed in an earth billions of years old, with the "days" of Genesis 1 representing long periods of time. He believed that life had gradually increased in complexity over vast periods of time, from single-cell organisms to the complexity of modern mammals and birds. But he believed these creatures came into being through distinct acts of creation.

All this was "strictly an academic exercise" for Rana, however, until he got a telephone call from his mother. He should come at once. His father was near death.

––––––––––

As Rana prepared for the long drive to West Virginia, the pent-up frustrations about his relationship with his father swept over him. He had never been able to talk to his father about matters of faith. He had given up trying, tired of the fighting it caused. He knew that his father had suffered, too, blaming himself for his son's conversion to a faith he considered irrational and superstitious. All these years had not softened his stubborn antagonism. Now Rana wondered whether it was too late to try again.

Two years before, a stroke had partially disabled his father. Since then, it had been difficult to communicate on any subject, let alone faith. Rana could only hope that his father would still be alive when he reached West Virginia. He could only hope that his father would be clear enough to have the conversation they should have had years ago. Rana knew he needed to truly engage his father. He needed to find a way to explain his faith. In the car Rana listened to a tape of C. S. Lewis's *Mere Christianity*, absorbing its message so that he could share it with his father if he got the chance.

When he reached the hospital, however, he soon saw that he had missed his chance. His father, though still clinging to life, was beyond conversation.

His failure to reach his father burned deeply into Rana. All the years when the opportunity had been there, he had been unable to take it. He had never equipped himself to explain his faith persuasively. Even though he had been growing in Christ, he had been unable to offer his highly rational father reasons why the Christian faith made sense. And now it was too late.

"I remember praying, 'God, I'm just a scientist, but I want you to use me for evangelism. I need to reach out so that people don't die like my father died, without knowing who you are.' I felt like I had dropped the ball in a major way. I had not taken my faith seriously. I had not treated it as a matter of life and death."

As Rana tried to make up for lost time, Hugh Ross's books were particularly helpful. Rana contacted Ross's apologetics ministry, Reasons to Believe, and signed up for a rigorous thirty-four-week training course. As he gained confidence, he became more open about his beliefs at work. A time of great excitement followed. Sometimes conversations in the hallways attracted crowds of interested people. Because of the interest generated by these discussions, Rana launched a Bible study where several of his colleagues came to faith.

Such evangelistic conversations soon became more important to Rana than his work. With his knowledge of biological systems, he felt that he had contributions to make—biological apologetics to supplement Ross's apologetics based on physics. When Rana read that Reasons to Believe was considering adding another scientist to its staff, he wrote the organization, offering his services. It would mean a complete change in lifestyle and a much lower salary. But if the door opened, he was ready to walk through it.

Hugh Ross left academic research and launched Reasons to Believe in 1986 at his pastor's encouragement. "I know you think this is normal," the pastor said after learning that Ross had helped lead three hundred strangers to Christ the year before, "but it's not common."

Ross could play an astronomer for a TV science program. He is as calm as a well and speaks in a voice from FM classical radio. Unusual for a scientist, though, Ross is an evangelist down to his toes. He came to faith as an adult through a highly rational process of investigation, and he means to pass on that same rational faith to everyone he meets. Ross is never fazed by a question. He offers authoritative answers—neat, incisive, with no room for a rejoinder. His approach is aimed at those Americans for whom science really matters. He talks their language. He communicates that he understands and values science, and that scientific evidence is inevitably the friend of faith.

For years Reasons to Believe (RTB) was Ross and his wife, Kathy, plus a cadre of volunteers. RTB has grown, but it remains a small organization with a handful of professional staff, headquartered in a nondescript two-story office building on a busy Southern California boulevard. The organization presents itself as a think tank on faith and science, and its literature is a lot more technical than what you'll find on most Christian apologetics websites.

Since joining Ross in 1999, Rana has published four books of biological apologetics and contributed many articles to the organization's website. His job involves keeping abreast of scientific literature and informing readers of any developments that have implications for Christian faith. He also speaks and debates occasionally.

Rana says that Ross has a prophetic style, while he, Rana, is more of a teacher. His manner is casual—he sports a goatee and favors blue jeans— and his answers tend to be longer and more complicated than Ross's. He is open to uncertainty. That probably makes his presentations more appealing to scientists but less appealing to laypeople seeking absolute clarity. Rana's books are far too technical for the ordinary nonscientist to appreciate. He writes clearly, but there are limits to how much he can or will simplify the science.

Ross was among the first Christians to popularize the fine-tuning of the universe for life, the so-called anthropic principle. For Ross, this is straightforward evidence for God. Such exquisitely tuned phenomena, and so many of them, could not be an accident. Our world was artfully designed for life.

Rana has attempted to show something similar for biology, using design. The biological design argument is hardly new. The brilliant eighteenth-century thinker William Paley articulated it most famously, comparing creation to a perfectly functioning watch. If the watch suggests the existence of a watchmaker, Paley said, then the creation suggests the existence of a creator.

"People have abandoned Paley way too quickly," Rana says. "Now everybody in apologetics is worried about defeating Darwinism. The crux of the arguments is negative: evolution can't explain complexity. I think there's a place for that kind of discussion, but you're saying that Darwinism is really the preferred explanation. Design is only worth considering once you've proven that [evolution] has failed. That's a bizarre position for a Christian."

Michael Behe is known for proclaiming the cell's irreducible complexity that could never be formed by chance. Rana points out how hard it is to prove a negative. If you say biochemistry is irreducibly complex, you can lose the argument to a single plausible counterexample.

Instead, Rana promotes a positive understanding of design. The cell looks designed; scientists treat it as designed. Scientists working in nanotechnology often investigate the structure of cells, trying to learn how to build effective nanosystems. In other words, they investigate God's designs in order to copy them. "They are implicitly operating on a design frame. Scientists have borrowed the capital of design and imported it into evolution. They talk about the cell's design and how clever it is. There's a teleological component just under the surface."

Rana agrees with Behe that the cell is irreducibly complex, but he would use that positively. Irreducible complexity is a typical characteristic of designed systems. Whenever you see it, you can rightly suspect that the system may have been designed. It's not a slam-dunk proof of the kind Behe attempts; rather it's "pattern recognition."

Exactly how God does his design work, Rana is not so ready to say. Some evolutionary creationists also embrace the language of design. They contend, however, that the designing was done through evolutionary processes.

Rana agrees that God works through natural processes. Creatures change by gradual evolution, and they may even separate into new species. But Rana's belief is that such processes don't innovate. Whenever you see something really new appearing in evolutionary history—whether mammals appearing for the first time or Adam and Eve appearing in Eden—it happens because God has intervened in an unusual way. "Whenever there is innovation there must be a creator stepping in and working outside of the process that he's instituted."

God works both directly and indirectly. "In Genesis 2 you read how God made Adam by fabricating him from dust, by breathing life into him. That sounds like direct, personal involvement. But in Genesis 1:3 God says, 'Let the light appear.' Clearly, God is involved, but he doesn't seem actively engaged in the same way."

It's the same throughout the Bible. Sometimes God works with his people through extremely personal encounters—as he did with Moses. Other times he uses forces—disease or war or weather—to move them. Rana thinks evolutionary creationists remove God's personal involvement too much.

When Rana talks about God's direct involvement in creation, he's making a very subtle distinction. "A patent lawyer said to me, 'When somebody invents something, what's the mechanism by which he invents it?' You could similarly ask, when God is intervening, what's the mechanism? There really isn't a mechanism as such. It's the idea." Much as lab scientists might manipulate a chemical environment to form something new, so God designs new life through creating conditions such that it can emerge.

Rana is humble talking about such philosophical and theological matters. That might be natural—he's not trained in these areas—but he's just as humble talking about science, where he is very knowledgeable indeed. It's his personality, partly—he's easygoing and naturally friendly. But it's also characteristic of him as a scientist. Science is provisional. Scientists offer explanations of how things work and give evidence for those explanations, but even before their explanations are offered to the public, they have to respond to critiques from their peers, often quite critical. Scientists know their ideas will be debated and tested by others, and they expect that their understanding will be modified as more is understood. (When the occasional scientist poses as a philosopher, he or she may make unqualified, sweeping assertions about what science has proved; but in their investigative work, scientists don't operate that way at all.)

Thus Rana sometimes admits that he might be proved wrong. For example, as National Institutes of Health director Francis Collins indicates in *The Language of God*, one important evidence for evolution is in the gene regulating vitamin C. Almost all creatures synthesize their own vitamin C, which is necessary for life. Humans and a few other creatures—notably chimpanzees, our nearest relatives according to evolutionary theory—do not. Humans need to get vitamin C in their diet, or they get scurvy (as sailors did before the nineteenth century when they went on long sea voyages without fresh food). What is interesting, however, is that when scientists decoded the genome, they found that humans and chimpanzees actually possess the gene for synthesizing vitamin C in the same position that other mammals have it. The only difference is that the human (and chimp) gene is broken. It would seem that in their branch of the evolutionary tree, a mutation made the gene go wrong, leaving its broken evidence behind.

Rana admits it's strong evidence for evolution, and he doesn't have an alternative explanation. But "given how much has happened with junk DNA, I'm not willing to give up yet."

When scientists first began to understand the molecular basis of genetics, they discovered huge amounts of what some called *junk DNA*—coding in the genome that didn't seem to do anything. This was a great challenge to creationists like Rana, because those strands of extra DNA seemed to be genetic fossils, leftovers from an evolutionary past that had no present value at all. Lately, though, to Rana's relief, some of those extra strands have been reclaimed as showing function in regulating other genes. Few talk about junk DNA anymore.

"I think there is a lot more to be discovered," Rana says, "and I'd like to let things play out. Our view of the genome is going to be radically different ten years from today. We want to be careful about being premature in drawing conclusions. We're in the middle of an avalanche. Let's wait for the dust to settle."

Rana expects that science will continue to learn more and that eventually he could be proved wrong—or right. There's fluidity in his thinking that's characteristic of science—an ongoing, back-and-forth, communal search for understanding.

———

In all the controversy over human evolution, the origins of the first cell often get overlooked. Rana (with coauthor Hugh Ross) has devoted a whole book to the subject, *Origins of Life*. He chronicles the failure of scientists to come up with a plausible explanation of how life might have sprung spontaneously from chemicals. Lots of people have the vague idea that scientists understand how chemicals in a hot soup probed by lightning generated life, but no plausible explanation exists. All avenues of exploration have failed.

"Origin-of-life research is not in its infancy. It's been going for fifty years. Stanley Miller published his paper [famously proposing a chemical model for the formation of simple life] the same year as Watson and Crick [discovered the structure of DNA]. In one there has been revolution after revolution; in the other there has been not a lot of progress, despite a lot of creativity brought to the problem."

Characteristically, though, Rana does not focus on the failure of evolutionary science to explain the origins of life. Rather, he takes a positive approach. Rana is quite confident that scientists will soon create life in a test tube. He's a great admirer of the scientists working to do so. "It's sheer brilliance. I have nothing but admiration for the people doing synthetic biology. It's what I would want to do if I could get a lab." In a very short time he expects to see new living organisms produced, unlike anything that exists in nature, using synthetic components.

That prospect would alarm many creationists because it would seem to eliminate the Creator's uniqueness. To Rana, however, "it's a new design argument. New life requires a designer. There's no way the lab conditions could be done on planet Earth. Scientists set up conditions so that chemistry happens. They manipulate nature in a very precise way."

If one categorizes the various schools of thought about creation, Reasons to Believe falls under intelligent design. It emphasizes the design-made aspect of creation and doubts the adequacy of unguided evolution to leap the stairs of increased complexity required to produce life.

Usually, intelligent design is closely associated with Michael Behe's network of friends and associates, the "secret cell" once connected through

Phillip Johnson. The Discovery Center in Seattle has become the institutional embodiment of this group.

But Reasons to Believe is not connected to the Discovery Center, and it represents ID in a very different way. Part of the difference is tone: it doesn't have all the answers and doesn't pretend to. But this difference in tone also has practical implications. For example, Rana and Ross insist that ID has no place (yet) in the school curriculum. This stand has infuriated some of their supporters, but they stick to it. Their reasoning is simple, if subtle. Seeing themselves as missionaries to the science community, they want to speak in the language of science. And science is an elite endeavor, where truth is not debated by amateurs.

"We are trained as scientists," Rana says, "and we had careers as scientists before we went into ministry. We understand how science is done, how scientists think. A lot of Christians don't understand, and as a result they are offensive to scientists. Christians come along with a challenge to evolution. Their critique has some merit, and they can show evidence for design. But the science community will say, 'This isn't science. Where is your model?'

"People are highly dismissive of that. They say, 'These guys are trying to avoid the evidence. They are evasive.' They fail to realize, the model is everything in science."

Those critiquing evolution must offer an alternative explanation of how things came to be. If not evolution, then what? It's not enough to say God did it. Science studies *how*. A genuine model enables scientists to make predictions that can be tested.

"I don't know that the ID community has ever really delivered on that. If they had kept the discussion at the academic level, it might be different." Instead some ID proponents attacked the science being taught in schools and suggested that ID deserved to be taught as an alternative science. "The scientific community reacted violently against that."

Trying to get scientists to listen, Reasons to Believe produces heady materials. Its leaders try to make their arguments in the form of a scientific model, with predictions that can be tested over time. They listen carefully to those who criticize them, and they seek interaction.

"What we offer is very provisional. Some people don't like that. They want the answer. But for us, it's more of a conversation."

7 Mary Schweitzer
Digging Dinosaurs

Mary Schweitzer has all the qualities to become a media star in the glamorous field of dinosaur paleontology. Attractive and articulate, with long light-brown hair, she carries herself with the easy grace of a Montanan who lives outdoors.

She went back to school while her three children were still in grade school. She had no ambitions for fame or even for a career, she says, wanting nothing more than to raise children and ultimately welcome grandchildren at their mountain home. Out of curiosity, however, she wanted to learn about dinosaurs. As a girl, she had found them fascinating, though her knowledge had not been upgraded since reading *The Enormous Egg*.

When she went to ask permission to audit a Montana State University class with famed paleontologist Jack Horner, a consultant for the movie *Jurassic Park*, she told him honestly that she was a young earth creationist.

"Well, I'm an atheist," he said, shaking hands. "Have a seat."

A few years later she was his graduate student, studying the weight-bearing bone structure of fossils from *Tyrannosaurus rex*. Horner pioneered a new kind of paleontology that looks at the microscopic internal structure of fossils.

Schweitzer's study required thin-slicing the fossil so that light could pass through it. She had difficulties in preparing her samples, so she asked for help from a woman she knew in the veterinary department of Montana State University, an expert in bone histology. This woman went to a veterinary conference to give a talk. In the question segment after her presentation, someone asked what was the oldest bone with which she had ever worked. Remembering that she had brought one of Schweitzer's samples of a *T. rex* femur, she projected the slide on the screen. After the session was over, a member of the audience approached her to say, "Do you realize you've got red blood cells in that dinosaur bone?"

When Schweitzer's veterinary friend showed her what they had seen, she was flabbergasted. "I got goose bumps." There were indeed little reddish circles in the cross section of bone, right in the channels where blood vessels had run. But nobody was going to credit a graduate student who claimed to have discovered sixty-million-year-old fossilized red blood cells. Schweitzer wanted a tidy thesis, not a boatload of controversy. As her mentor Horner would write, "She did not feel ready for this kind of attention. It was a bit like being called up from the minor leagues to pitch in Yankee Stadium when you weren't sure you had control of your curveball yet."[1]

Consequently, she said nothing about it to Horner. She canvassed other graduate students while trying to make sense of what she had. Horner heard the gossip, however, and called her in.

She showed up at his office at nine, and he kept her waiting until ten thirty. He was furious. "What gave you the right to take my bone anywhere?" he wanted to know and went off on a forty-five-minute rant. At the conclusion, having vented himself, he asked to see her sample. There followed a ten-minute silence. Little red orbs were unmistakable. Some even had visible nuclei.

"So what do you think they are?" he finally asked.

"They look like blood cells," she answered.

"Prove to me that they are not."

For the next two years Schweitzer used every trick of chemistry to test the samples. She says she is still not able to say without a doubt that they are blood cells. But she can't say they aren't either. She has clear evidence that parts of hemoglobin molecules survive in the fossils, with no corresponding chemicals in the surrounding rock. The only explanation seems to be blood.

Fame had come to find her. She had opened unthinkable possibilities, that fossilization could preserve soft tissues. Everyone had assumed that fossils were of hard stuff like bones and teeth and occasionally impressions left by skin or leaves. How could something as delicate as blood cells survive sixty million years? Her accidental finding raised the question of just what a fossil really was.

It was a stunning discovery that rippled throughout the world of paleontology. And it would not be the last time that Mary Schweitzer astonished the world. Others would give a lot for her fame, Mary Schweitzer says. But hating the limelight as she does, she would be glad to do without it.

———

Schweitzer loves Montana, the state where she was born and raised, and seems to begrudge every moment spent elsewhere. Her father owned a furniture store in Helena. Unusual for a small-town Montana businessman, he was an avid reader and a somewhat mystical and broad-minded Roman Catholic. While her relationship to her mother was sometimes strained, Schweitzer adored her father and followed him on his fly-fishing excursions. She was terribly tall and shy and doesn't remember having any friends at school, but with her father she could talk about anything. "I was probably his best friend, and he mine."

A much older brother went off to Catholic University in Washington, DC, planning to be a priest. When she was five, he sent her books. Some of the books were about dinosaurs—*The Enormous Egg*, about a boy who finds an egg that hatches into a triceratops, and *The Shy Stegosaurus.*

That led to nothing, however. Math terrified Schweitzer, and she avoided the sciences through high school. "I wasn't smart enough" to be a scientist, she says. In any case, girls could only grow up to be secretaries or maybe nurses.

When she was sixteen, Schweitzer went to her first meeting of Young Life, an evangelical Christian organization that held home meetings aiming to introduce high school students to Jesus. She was transfixed. Her father greeted her when she arrived home, and they stayed up late talking. "Wow," she told him, "I saw a side of God I didn't know existed." God had been an important touchstone in her life, but "all of a sudden he became three-dimensional. There he was. I could touch him and see him. He just got big." It was the difference, she says, between knowing about a subject and knowing it for yourself.

Two nights later she woke up to go to the bathroom and noticed lights on in the rest of the house. She heard sobbing. She heard the voice of a neighbor. Thoroughly alarmed, she ran down the stairs, screaming. Her father, she learned, had died of a heart attack.

That night "had a profound effect on me. I cried so hard, and then I never cried again. I became angry. I didn't deal with my emotions." Devastated, her mother went into a world of her own. The leaders in Young Life became Schweitzer's emotional and spiritual lifeline, supporting her and leading her deeper into a loving relationship with God. "If it hadn't been for Young Life, I would have been so bitter. I would have gone off the deep end."

Schweitzer had planned to go out of state for college, but she knew she couldn't leave her mother. Attending college a short drive away in

Bozeman, she experienced devastating loneliness until she found a new faith community.

She took a class in speech therapy and loved it. It was a practical way to help people who were very deeply in need. Eventually, she finished her degree in speech and hearing science at Utah State.

Schweitzer's life changed drastically after graduation. She went home to Helena, where she reconnected with a man she had dated in Bozeman. They soon married, and five months later she was pregnant. In four years she had three kids.

She wasn't ready for it. "I felt isolated and incompetent, staying at home raising kids. I had nobody to talk to. I didn't know anybody." She and her husband had moved back to Bozeman, where he was involved in building a business. Church offered some community, but not enough.

Looking for refuge, she began to take classes at Montana State. She had no degree in mind; she attended for personal stimulation, even though at first she found it terrifying. Almost thirty, raising three kids, she felt out of place with younger students. But she took a creative writing class and found herself liberated. "It was amazing. I could be me."

After taking a smattering of classes in various subjects, she decided to prepare for medical school. It fit with her family. Her brother was now a doctor; her mother was a nurse. Premed pushed her into intimidating classes: physics and organic chemistry. She found that she could do the work. She took the MCAT (Medical College Admission Test) and did well but then realized she had reached a dead end. Montana had no medical school, so she would have to go to Seattle if she wanted to pursue medicine. She couldn't leave her kids, and her husband's job wasn't portable.

Instead of going to medical school, she gained her certificate to teach high school science. She signed up to be a substitute teacher, and then, sad to be finished with school, settled down to wait and see what would happen.

———————

While she waited, Schweitzer decided it would be interesting to audit Jack Horner's class on paleontology. She knew there were conflicts with the young earth creationism she had been taught in church and Young Life, but she was curious enough to overlook that.

For their first class, Horner brought a box of fossils. Rather than lecture the class, he asked the students to examine the fossils and tell him what they saw. In his approach, science was all about evidence.

Schweitzer learned about dinosaurs in the class, but she also learned about science. "Scientists are going with what they see. I was learning how science is done, how scientists ask questions. Everything is testable. Everything can be proved wrong." As she dealt with evidence from multiple fields, Schweitzer's young earth creationism soon fell away. "The earth is six thousand years old? What evidence do you have for that? If your salvation doesn't hinge on it, don't make a big deal out of it."

Horner was a demanding and intimidating teacher who got mad if his students answered wrong. "He pushed all my buttons." At the same time, he was proudly unconventional and willing to take a chance on a nontraditional student like Schweitzer. "He gave me the opportunity to sink or swim."

She swam because she fell passionately in love with the subject. "When I held my first dinosaur fossil, I thought, *This was alive.* The awe of it was phenomenal." On her first field trip she found a dinosaur fossil and realized that she was looking at something no human being had ever seen.

"I love dinosaurs. I can use my [academic] tools for any creatures, but I don't want to do the work if I'm not interested." Paleontology, Schweitzer says, is a unique field, with "no money and an inordinate press. There are a lot of weirdos in the field, and I am one of them. I can't imagine doing anything else."

Seized by her interest and unable to go on extensive field trips because of her young children, Schweitzer became a volunteer at the Museum of the Rockies in Bozeman. There she helped to prepare and preserve dinosaur fossils coming in to the museum, including the recently discovered MOR 555, the most complete *Tyrannosaurus rex* ever found. At the museum Schweitzer became acquainted with many of the researchers and their work. She was full of questions—"nine million questions, questions every day." An exasperated Horner told her, "Go figure it out yourself. Go to graduate school."

When Schweitzer talks about this period of her life, she is a bundle of contradictory feelings. She was discovering her passion for dinosaurs, her life's work. It was not easy to combine her delight in science with her life as a wife and mother.

After six months of wavering, Schweitzer proceeded to grad school. She took extra jobs as a medical transcriber and a teaching assistant to pay for tuition. At the same time she fulfilled her responsibilities as a wife and mother. "I never missed a soccer game or a dentist appointment. I washed and ironed. I baked bread from scratch. I mowed the lawn." But her heart was elsewhere. "My kids are the most important thing on the planet to me, but I don't think they got that message. I fulfilled the written requirements but not the spirit. If I had the faith I have now, I would make different choices. I had little Christian input. I got lazy in my faith."

Some of that breakdown came because her Christian friends, all young earth creationists, couldn't engage with what she was learning. They weren't interested in science and were doubtful of a field that dealt in creatures tens of millions of years old. Schweitzer felt alone in graduate school, where she didn't fit with either the professors or the other grad students. She felt equally lonely in church and at home.

That she completed her PhD studies in four years is a testimony to her dogged work. Shortly thereafter, in 1997, she published two academic papers based on her research. Her findings were controversial—it remained unthinkable to many that red blood cells could be preserved in fossilized form—but also sensational. Ironically, some of the greatest buzz came from young earth creationists, who "argued that since we had thought that such things couldn't be preserved and now had found they were preserved to some extent, that meant our dating was wrong," as Horner wrote. According to Schweitzer, though, the age of the fossils, based on many lines of evidence, wasn't in doubt. What came under question was the "conventional wisdom that no biological materials like hemoglobin or red blood cells could survive as fossils."[2] The models of fossil formation needed rethinking.

Given her dramatic findings, Schweitzer might have been recruited to teach at other prestigious schools, but that wasn't possible given her family responsibilities. Montana State didn't hire its own graduates, so a professor's job there wasn't going to happen. She continued her research with postdoctoral grants and occasional teaching. "I never dreamed of my own lab."

———

Four years later Schweitzer's life fell apart when she and her husband divorced. Schweitzer doesn't talk about this much. The experience was devastating; she feels she lost almost everything most precious to her. At the same time, it drove her closer to God and deeper in her faith. "I had no pride left, which is the best thing in the world."

Out of necessity she moved out of the house that she and her husband had built. She withdrew from people in order to read and pray. "For three months I railed and whined." At the bottom of her pain, however, she found solid rock.

"Please, God," she prayed, "don't let me be bitter." God answered that prayer, she says. "Mostly, God helped me. I learned to ask for forgiveness" without demanding any quid pro quo. She "got a flavor of what it cost

Jesus to be falsely accused and not to answer." She learned to look for good in even the worst situation. "As soon as you make that choice, God will bless you." Dallas Willard, C. S. Lewis, John Townsend, and Henry Cloud were some of the most helpful authors. She found her life verse, Genesis 50:20: "God intended it for good."

She realized that she was no longer tied to Bozeman. Her children were nearly grown and didn't need her full-time anymore. Besides, she needed a job. A position opened at North Carolina State. She applied for it and was hired.

The move was daunting; she sobbed all through the flight to Raleigh-Durham. She didn't want to live anywhere but Montana or to operate on her own. The challenge of designing courses, overseeing graduate students, and setting up her own laboratory loomed large. At times, she was so lonely and distraught she wasn't sure she could survive. "I remember virtually nothing about the first six months there," she says.

In the middle of this emotional turbulence, while setting up her new laboratory, Schweitzer pulled out a small box she had carried with her, filled with fossil fragments. The box had a story behind it. In 2000, researchers from Montana State had searched for fossils in the Hell Creek Formation of eastern Montana. They found five *T. rex* specimens, a rich haul. One of them, discovered on a forty-foot cliff face, was a nearly complete skeleton. Three years and many jackhammers were required to free it from the rock. When they had it out, the location was so remote only a helicopter could carry it to a road. Unfortunately, the femur, encased in rock and plaster, was so heavy the helicopter could not lift it. They had to break it into two pieces to get it out. In making the break, some fragments came loose. They had not been painted with chemicals to preserve them, which meant that they were chemically uncorrupted compared to almost all dinosaur samples. The researchers gave the bone fragments to Schweitzer for her studies. She packed them up and took them with her to North Carolina.

Now, in her new laboratory, she opened the box for the first time and pulled out a fist-size fragment of bone. "My gosh," she said. "It's a girl, and it's pregnant."

In all the many studies of dinosaur fossils, a sure identification of gender and pregnancy had never been made. Schweitzer drew this conclusion because she had been studying ostrich bone. According to evolutionary theory, birds are direct descendants of dinosaurs. Birds have very light, thin bones in order to fly. Unlike, say, mammalian bones, avian bones store a very limited amount of calcium. This creates a problem when they prepare to lay eggs because eggshells require significant amounts of calcium. Because of this, birds respond to ovulation by laying down a special type of tissue in their bone, medullary bone. It lasts only a short time, while they are laying. It has a distinctive structure, easily identified. When Schweitzer looked at the *T. rex* bone, she saw that structure. Subsequent tests confirmed that it was, indeed, identical to medullary bone as seen in modern birds. She had identified a female dinosaur about to lay eggs.

Schweitzer had yet more discoveries in store. She wanted to etch a piece of the bone, removing some minerals in order to study the bone structure. That meant putting the bone in acid for a brief time. Her lab technician took on the project, then came to Schweitzer in alarm. The bone had dissolved too quickly; at first she thought it was all gone. Then she discovered that something was left: something that rebounded like a rubber band when she pulled on it with tweezers, a tissue that stretched, twisted, folded. It looked for all the world like collagen, a protein that forms the basis of most bone and connective tissue.

Schweitzer proceeded to do similar experiments on cortical bone. What was left behind looked like "fragments of tubing, very, very small tubing." It, too, was flexible.

"You're not going to believe this," her laboratory technician said, "but I think we have blood vessels."

"You're right," Schweitzer said. "I don't believe this. Nobody's going to believe this. We can't talk about this."

"I don't think either one of us slept for three weeks. We kept repeating and repeating and repeating our experiments."[3]

"That was a Eureka moment. Very scary."

On top of that, using a microscope Schweitzer found in the *T. rex* bone the "unmistakable outline of the cells that make bones grow—osteocytes.

"She called me up," wrote Horner, "to say she had found osteocytes. I assumed she meant the spaces where the osteocytes would have been."

"'No, Jack, actually we have the cells and they have filopodia and they have nuclei.'"[4]

Science published Schweitzer's discoveries in 2005, creating a sensation in the world of paleontology. (Subsequent papers came out in 2007.) The media, always fascinated by dinosaurs, featured her work, not always with the seriousness and care that Schweitzer would have appreciated. She is very sensitive to publicity. She knows that the public supports her work through taxes, and she feels a responsibility to explain what she does to the waitress who gives a percentage of her tips to pay for expensive labs to study dinosaur fossils. Even so, Schweitzer would like to be left in peace. She never sought fame; it found her. She simply wants to do her research.

––––––––––

Schweitzer represents a third wave of dinosaur research. Wave one was bones, with skeletons fitted together and put on display in museums. By studying the bones' shapes and sizes and the places where tendons had attached, paleontologists put together a catalog of hundreds of species of dinosaurs and how they lived.

Jack Horner and others initiated a second wave, looking at the interior structure of the fossils using microscopes and other tools of analysis. Schweitzer and others have taken this to a third stage, doing chemical analysis. Molecules are fossils, too, these researchers say, transformed by time but nonetheless retaining remnants of the past. Schweitzer has discovered what appear to be organic molecules hidden in dinosaur fossils. Analyzing these is a complex, expensive matter.

She despairs of funding. Often she wonders whether it will be possible to continue her work, considering how few grants are available and how difficult it is to obtain them. Grad students depend on continuing funding, and "if I lose my technician, I'm done. I have to trust God. It's up to him. If he's closing this door, I will look for something else." It's hard to imagine Schweitzer doing anything else.

She is passionate about science and passionate about God. Schweitzer belongs to conservative churches that believe in a young earth. She leans heavily on these congregations, who trust in the Bible and offer her spiritual nurture. "We don't have to be on the same page if we have Jesus at the core of our friendship."

She did draw the line at a pastor who, not knowing who she was, preached about her discovery of red blood cells as an indication of the stupidity of scientists. "I got up and left. If you can't do your homework on something as simple as that, why should I believe you on spiritual things? If you are going to rely on just one source, how do I know what you do with the Bible?"

"I have few close friends who are scientists," Schweitzer says. "I can only let walls down with those who share my faith." Friendships with fellow Christians are not without tensions. "Many of my friends are praying for my enlightenment." But she also sympathizes with the stresses affecting young earth creationists.

Many of the North Carolina State undergraduates who take her course, Dinosaur World, come from conservative churches. "They see the data for evolution, and they are placed in an uncomfortable position, splitting their heads and their hearts. They usually choose to walk away from their faith."

Some come privately to her with their questions. "I tell them that the world might indeed be six thousand years old, just as dinosaurs might have had purple polka dots, but without data you can't say that." She wants them to grasp the authority of science in its proper area but also the limits of science. "The best gift I can give my students is to ask the right questions. I tell them that science is not the only answer. Science can't prove the existence of God or that you love your children. There's so much that we can't touch with science because science is meant to be measured. You can't measure God.

"It's a false chasm. You don't have to choose between science and faith." She cites her experience when she first recognized the strength of the case for an ancient earth. "I could have gone away from my faith, but I knew God."

She also tells them that she doesn't have all the answers. She could be wrong. Yet she doesn't think so. The reality of the fossils, which she knows so well, tells a different story. In Argentina, she visited dinosaur nesting sites running for ten miles along ancient riverbanks. The nests are in layers four deep, successive floods having deposited new sediments that dinosaurs inhabited. Maybe there is a way to explain this as a product of Noah's great flood at the dawn of human history, but Schweitzer doubts it.[5]

She believes there is room in the Bible for an old earth once populated with dinosaurs. "Let God be God," she likes to say.

8 Darrel Falk
Putting the Pieces Back Together

An intensely shy and serious child, Darrel Falk grew up with a reputation among his friends for never lying or swearing. Following his parents' lead he asked Jesus into his heart at the age of four, and through an altar call at the age of ten he experienced (in the holiness language of his upbringing) a second work of grace. "I feel so clean inside," he said afterward in tearful wonder.

People in his family's small Nazarene church near Vancouver, British Columbia, were different from everybody else he knew. They didn't dance, swear, or go to movies; the women didn't use makeup; and they didn't think about life as other people did. "I went for years knowing only a handful of people who believed in the sort of God whom we believed in." This difference was often a strength: Falk found great security in his community. "I grew up in a wonderful church and family."

As an introspective child given to worry, Falk occasionally wondered whether Christianity was too good to be true. "I wanted it to be true because it was so beautiful. Jesus was my best friend. I felt very close to God." He kept doubts deeply buried. "I didn't want anybody to know I had them, lest they think I was a bad person."

Nevertheless, doubts sometimes surfaced: "I questioned how it could be that, given all the religions in the world (including, especially, the religion of no religion), I was fortunate enough to have been born into the right one."[1] Such questions went unaddressed; they had a radioactive character that he tried to shield from his mind.

In junior high he encountered a textbook that pictured humans evolving from apes. "The images of those charts of human evolution in my seventh-grade social studies textbook are still etched on my mind. They almost cost me my Christian faith." He didn't believe evolution was true—his church read Genesis with a strict literalism—but he feared it might be and that his faith would be undone. "The following summer, at a church camp, I spoke to a couple of friends, both of whom were sixth graders. I told them that they would find the seventh grade to be enormously challenging to their belief in God. 'You are going to be hearing about the Cro-Magnon humans, the Neanderthals, and the evolution of the human race. Be prepared for an assault on your faith,' I told them. I felt fortunate to have emerged from seventh grade with mine intact."[2]

He heard no antievolution sermons; he knew of no books or magazines that addressed the rift he perceived between science and the Bible. The problem seemed to be his and his alone, and he dealt with it mainly by not thinking about it.

———

Falk's parents were not highly educated—his father attended just one year of Bible college—but seeing that Falk was an excellent student, they wanted him to attend university. He was particularly good at math and science, sticking to chemistry and physics and deliberately avoiding biology for fear that it would test his faith. His one high school biology class never talked about evolution or DNA.

After a year at a church Bible college, where he met his future wife, Falk started at Vancouver's Simon Fraser University, commuting from home by bus. He had decided to become a doctor, which meant he could no longer steer clear of biology. His first semester required Biology 101. His second semester found him enrolled in three courses: intro to biology, genetics, and developmental biology. He hoped that his Bible college studies had prepared him for an intellectual test of faith.

He was completely unprepared for the beauty he encountered. "I had known the beauty of Christianity. Now I discovered the beauty of genetics. When I saw how the cell worked, it was unbelievably beautiful. Thousands of protein molecules, intricately folded, each doing a particular job in the cell. This astonishing process was going on in every one of my trillions of cells, making me who I am. Forty years later, I'm still in love with it. It never gets old, never loses its appeal."

> Learning for the first time about what seemed to me a magical world, the world of DNA, RNA and protein synthesis, was the most exhilarating intellectual experience of my life. . . . I had never imagined that anything could be so elegant as the orchestrated dances that take place inside microscopic cells. The process of protein synthesis seemed to me more beautiful than the most glorious ballet. The living processes of a single cell, and the unfolding and coordination of the plan for a developing embryo, were like a magnificent symphony, and I felt that I would never be able to find greater intellectual joy than I would by spending the rest of my life studying its orchestration.[3]

His career plans changed. He began to aim for a life in scientific research.

Initially, the beauty of the cell encouraged his faith. "It became increasingly difficult to believe that chance and natural selection, apart from God's initial design and providential oversight, could have built the wondrous processes I was studying. Hence, for the first time, I began to see that my faith and intellect might not need to be kept in separate compartments."

He also discovered that biologists were not "plotting how best to overthrow Christian principles; they were simply individuals who loved doing experiments and getting answers."[4]

In other ways, however, faith and science were not so easily harmonized. Evidence that all life is related was clearly written in the cell. Every organism used the same molecules, the same proteins, the same assembly processes. Even for creatures as different as birds and sea slugs, grass and elephants, similarities at the molecular level jumped out at him. These were surely family resemblances.

He read Genesis 1 as a six-day history that he could not fit with what enthralled him in the laboratory. Though this difficulty made no immediate impact, his inability to imagine a way to resolve it undermined his confidence in the Bible as God's authoritative word. The difficulty didn't come from a church pushing literalism on him; it came from his internal sense of what the Bible said.

Though this conflict introduced doubts, Falk did not experience a slide away from faith until later, when he went on to do his PhD at the University of Alberta. The cause wasn't principally science. He and his wife attended a church that attracted young people questioning elements of their fundamentalist backgrounds. "Evolution was a side issue. We were questioning everything. Much of the questioning was healthy in others' cases, but not in mine." Issues that now seem small loomed large at the time. "I was bitter because I didn't go to my high school prom. We had missed out on going to movies. We had been isolated from the rest of society."

The Bible's deep wisdom might have helped Falk to enlarge and redefine the faith of his childhood, but due to unresolved issues with science, he had lost faith in the Bible's perspicuity. "Eventually, there wasn't much left of the classical Christianity of my youth."

Falk's two daughters were born while he was in graduate school. The second, he remembers, came into the world just six months before he was due to finish his PhD. Their lives would ultimately bend him toward a renewal of faith. But at the time they were born, he was far from God.

———————

Falk took his first postdoctorate at the University of British Columbia, in his old hometown of Vancouver. His mentor was David Suzuki, a famous geneticist who worked with fruit flies and would later become a renowned environmentalist and cultural commentator. Suzuki's lab was "very much a product of the sixties," attracting culturally adventurous scientists interested in the world outside the laboratory walls.

They were still expected to do laboratory science, however. When Falk's experiments didn't go well, it came as a rude shock. "I thought I was going to be a great geneticist," he says. "I was far too confident in myself." Instead, he faced the utter wreckage of procedures that didn't yield results. It is a reality every scientist encounters. Many are devastated when they first realize that—unlike lab experiments in high school or college—no one can tell them how to correct their errors. Nobody knows why things have gone wrong. It is up to them. They might never get their experiments to work.

Falk became very upset and discouraged. "I loved genetics, but I was far too interested in what people thought of my work. I didn't have much left when people didn't think I was smart." He sank into despondency.

Looking back, he sees those failures as crucial to his growth. "I really needed that crack in my ego. I needed to know that life is not about getting the applause of other people."

The rock opera *Jesus Christ Superstar* opened in Vancouver during that time, attracting interest among some of Falk's fellow scientists. One day Falk overheard them discussing it in the department lounge. They were interested in what the play said about Jesus and were pooling their meager knowledge. Unexpectedly, one of them turned to Falk, who was known to be a Christian, and asked, "Who were his disciples? Can you name them?"

"I had the strangest sensation when he turned to me, because I recognized that although there was a time when Jesus was my best friend, now he was not only *not* my best friend but he was even on the verge of becoming a distant memory. I had not opened my Bible in months and had not engaged in serious devotional study for a couple of years. . . . I had no right to be consulted as a person who knew anything more about Jesus than anyone else."[5]

Suddenly he realized how much he missed a relationship with the living God. Shaken by the realization that he had lost his faith, Falk was wrenched by the thought of his daughters, ages one and three. "I felt sad for them, that I wasn't going to be a good father to them, giving them what I had been given. I was twenty-seven years old, and I said to myself, 'This is not what I want.' I didn't want to be a bystander in faith anymore. I wanted to be a Christian again."

A few days later, seemingly by coincidence, a Christian professor in another department invited him to lunch. He encouraged Falk that faith and learning were meant to grow together. He went further, inviting Falk to come to his church and talk to his Sunday school class about developments in genetics. It was an act of life-changing kindness, reaching out to Falk to draw him back into the community. It was "my first step back."

Falk recognized that he had a long distance to travel, however. Concerns about evolution had not led directly to his loss of faith, but they now posed a major obstacle to reclaiming it. Could he put the Bible and his life in genetics together? He had great doubts.

One evening Falk closed the door to his bedroom and, just as he had been taught to do as a child, knelt by his bed to pray. He offered a classic doubter's prayer, telling God he was not even sure that he was there or that he heard prayers. "But I come on the basis of faith and am going to try living as though you are real again."

From that day, his faith began to grow. Falk found Christian books that expressed faith in a far deeper way than anything he had previously read or heard. Malcolm Muggeridge and Dietrich Bonhoeffer were particularly helpful; so were Leo Tolstoy and Mother Teresa. "It changed my life."

He could not see his way back to church, however. Occasionally he attended, but he found churches either theologically liberal and impersonal, or narrow and anti-intellectual. In the one he missed the warmth and devotion that he treasured from his childhood; in the other he felt sure he would always be viewed with suspicion. "I wanted Christian community. I was longing for it and for my family. But I wasn't going to be able to feel at home. I would always be an outsider."

He took a second postdoctoral fellowship in Southern California. On one memorable day he was at the beach with his family when he saw a church bus arrive in the parking lot. From the lettering on the side he could see the bus came from a Nazarene church, the denomination of his boyhood. "This church family, I reasoned, was having a picnic, just like I used to love so much." The sight prompted deep sadness as he thought of his daughters. They would never go on a church picnic. They would never gain the richest part of his heritage.

"I longed to go back, if only for the sake of my daughters. But I could not go back—the chasm that separated us was too great. One of the widest sections of the gulf was my belief in gradual creation."[6]

From his research position in Southern California, Darrel Falk gained a tenure-track professor's position at Syracuse University. This constituted real success in the world of genetic research. But he continued lonely in his reviving faith. Among the entire Syracuse faculty, he encountered very few Christians. He and his wife visited several churches but found nothing that offered the personal warmth and deep devotion they craved.

Evangelical churches seemed anti-intellectual and terribly literalistic with Scripture.

Discouraged, they all but gave up. As a last-ditch effort, Falk drove across town one Sunday morning to visit a small Nazarene church he knew of. Six months before that, he and his wife had driven to this church, not to go inside but just to park on the street and watch people leaving. They had seen people taking time to speak warmly; they had noticed two girls about the same ages as their own—were they the pastor's daughters? *Maybe we can go*, they thought. But as the week went on they decided, no, they shouldn't get their hopes up. There was too much pain in the thought of rejection.

Falk went alone, like a spy.

After the service, friendly faces surrounded him. The members acted delighted that he was a professor at Syracuse. Falk went home and told his wife, "We might have a church after all."

So it proved to be. Though the church certainly didn't believe in evolution, the members never bothered about the fact that Falk did. "That church—God's gift to us—built a bridge to us and welcomed us just as we were, gradual creation perspective and all."[7] The pastor helped Falk as he found his way to a fuller, more robust faith, eventually asking him to teach a Sunday school class for young adults. "I grew tremendously teaching Peter." Falk also worked hard, though unsuccessfully, to assemble a Christian fellowship among faculty and grad students at Syracuse. He longed to see the chapel of this historically Methodist institution become a place of worship again. He never did.

Continuing to work on the developmental genetics of the fruit fly, he gained tenure. He loved teaching. Gradually, though, he began to long to teach in a Christian community. There were so few Christians among the faculty, and the partying lifestyle he observed among students dismayed him. He knew he wouldn't want his daughters to attend such a school. Falk increasingly saw the significance of Christian education in a setting that valued teaching more than research.

Having become a board member in his church, he was praying and fasting for the congregation when he sensed the Lord speaking, almost audibly: "Darrel, you're not going to be here much longer. Go ahead and see if there is an opening in a Christian college."

It was a dramatic decision, to leave a well-known research institution. He wrote to many schools, and only one made an offer: Mount Vernon Nazarene in Ohio. Falk remembers a Mount Vernon Nazarene faculty member speaking at faculty devotions one Monday morning, mentioning with genuine humility that he was not at an important university. "'Here I am at this tiny Christian college,' he said, 'not a leading scholar, not contributing in any major way.' I remember thinking, *You don't know what you have. What you do in a Christian college setting is so much more important than anything I have seen in a research university.* He had only worked at Christian institutions and didn't know that what he experienced was the best of all. He had Christian community."

Falk was convinced that God had used gradual means over millions of years to develop life. The more science he learned, the more firmly established this conclusion appeared to him. Now that he had returned to full-hearted faith, he was also sure of the Bible's authority. He still didn't know exactly how to put those convictions together, though.

In conversation with a colleague in chemistry at Mount Vernon, Falk mentioned that he would someday like to write a book bringing science and faith together. "He said, 'The book has been written. It's called *Biology*. It's the introductory text we use in our course.'" Falk wasn't satisfied. He couldn't see why God was necessary by that scheme.

After four happy years at Mount Vernon Nazarene, Falk moved to Point Loma Nazarene in San Diego. Beginning in the summer of 1991, he joined in a multidisciplinary faculty discussion group that read books together and talked through many areas of faith and science. They read *Darwin on Trial* and *Darwin's Black Box*. They read Daniel Dennett's evolutionary atheism. They read Mark Noll's *Scandal of the Evangelical Mind*. They read Karl Barth. The dialogue was frank, sometimes painfully so. Falk and other science faculty learned from biblical scholars and theologians, who in turn absorbed biological science. Together, they worked toward faithfully bringing Scripture and science together.

During much of that discussion, Falk had a mind congenial to the emerging intelligent design community. "I was looking for gaps," parts of the creation story that science could not account for. When Phillip Johnson published *Darwin on Trial*, Falk picked it up eagerly, hoping for answers to his questions. The book disappointed him. It was clear that Johnson didn't know the science and "was putting in gaps that didn't exist." In meetings with ID advocates over the next ten years, Falk found them talking past him and vice versa. ID didn't produce anything he could recognize as scientifically worthwhile, and its advocates couldn't understand why scientists like him failed to grasp what seemed obvious to them. Had one of his science honors students produced the equivalent of Michael Behe's *Edge of Evolution*, Falk said, he was not sure it would have received a passing grade.

The faith-science dialogue at Point Loma produced no stunning insights for Falk, but it did introduce him to serious theology, particularly in the person of Karl Barth. "He was hard for someone like me to read, but Barth helped me see how deep theology could go." Stimulated, Falk stumbled on *Creation and Fall*, a small book from his old mentor Bonhoeffer. That showed him how rich the creation narrative was, how filled with meaning in God's salvation story.

Discussions also went on in the Nazarene denomination. At national meetings called to address issues of origins, Falk met other engaged colleagues. Several published books contributed to the discussion, notably those by Karl Giberson, a physicist at Eastern Nazarene. Although the subject was sensitive and controversial, Nazarene faculty members were anxious to engage it.

That was largely because they could see it mattered to students.

Those who came to Point Loma from Christian high schools had almost never learned about evolution. Those from public schools had studied origins only in a superficial way; they generally concluded, "Some people think that way, but they are wrong." Yet as these students learned the fundamentals of genetics and comparative anatomy, they would come to Falk's office and ask questions. Sometimes he and other faculty would host private discussion groups.

After years of such discussion, Falk felt that he should write a book aimed at students. He knew of nothing available from a biological perspective. And in biology, of course, lay the deepest questions.

Starting in 1995, Falk tried. He worked hard at his writing, but feedback he received from faculty and students suggested his samples were stiff and awkward. One student said reluctantly, "If you could only write like you can teach!" Falk put the project aside.

However, the subject did not go away. One day the university provost asked Falk to talk to a young earth creationist who was volunteering to teach science classes. Point Loma had no courses on either evolution or creation, and the volunteer teacher aggressively pushed to include young earth creationism in the curriculum. Falk suggested they meet occasionally and share perspectives.

It soon became obvious that the man wasn't interested in mere conversation. He was sending notes with his version of their talks to others, urging their concern over the deterioration of Point Loma Nazarene. Falk decided that the discussions were unproductive. Telling the man he was breaking off communication provoked an emotional reaction. "You're going to have to deal with this issue," the man said threateningly. "You won't be able to pussyfoot around it. A tidal wave is going to come and wash you all away."

Falk felt sure that the man was fundamentally right: the church *did* have to deal with the issue. Once again, Falk wished he had a careful, thoughtful book presenting what he believed. Rather than allow others to characterize his beliefs, he needed to lay them out. He went back to his writing. This time he kept in mind the student's comment. He pretended that he was in his classroom, answering questions that students posed.

When he had a manuscript, he offered it to students and faculty for their reaction. Most were positive, but one student showed it to a parent, who copied it. A friend of that parent sent it to denominational leaders and others. He wrote to the college's president with a series of accusations, demanding a response. Falk answered as graciously as he could. His critic was not satisfied; he turned Falk's words against him and accused Falk and Point Loma of deliberately destroying young people's faith.

Though he never met directly with his critic, Falk met with others concerned for the college's reputation: the man's pastor, the denomination's district superintendent, and the college's president and provost. All of them supported Falk's position, and for a time silence reigned.

But in the fall of 2000, the college president called in Falk and showed him a detailed, multiple-page letter from James Dobson, who had heard from the critics and was deeply concerned about the direction of Point Loma Nazarene. Dobson is a graduate of Point Loma (formerly Pasadena College). He had millions of followers through his role as a talk-show radio host. If he were to join an anti–Point Loma crusade, it could be disastrous for the school.

At the college president's urging, Falk composed an eleven- or twelve-page point-by-point response to Dobson's letter. "I felt that it was the most important thing I had ever done." For several months he heard little or nothing in response. Then the questions resurfaced. Phillip Johnson had been talking to Dobson, contending that Christian schools and their views on evolution should be exposed. Johnson invited Falk to a radio debate on Dobson's show.

"I declined the debate. Johnson is a Harvard-trained lawyer." But Falk suggested that a meeting could be arranged in which he could explain his position.

"The key accusation," Falk says, "was that I was destroying the faith of my students." He asked thirty-one students to write anonymously about the role of the biology department in their faith. Almost all wrote very positively. He showed those letters to Dobson. To Falk's great relief the meeting went well, ending in an embrace and a cordial agreement to disagree.

————

That is exactly what Falk pleads for in his book *Coming to Peace with Science*. He puts major emphasis on the doctrine of creation. Genesis 1–3 introduces the Bible's greater message, he points out: not only creation but new creation. Whether the language of Genesis is interpreted in a literal manner or in a figurative sense—Falk respectfully lays out alternative interpretations—the message must speak to our spiritual needs. To read it as a story of geology and biology alone would be to misread it terribly. The message of Genesis—indeed, of the whole Scripture—is a testimony to God's goodness, our need, and God's plan to save the world. "The full story of creation cannot be found in textbooks of biology, astronomy, physics or chemistry, because they provide only a hazy glimpse of creation's elegance."[8]

Falk lays out the evidence for an ancient earth and the gradual development of its creatures over millions of years. In simple layman's language he explains how scientists establish the age of the earth. He summarizes the fossil record and takes up creationist questions such as the purported lack of transitional fossils. He considers the geographical distribution of today's creatures and its evidences for gradual creation, and last takes up his area of special expertise, genetics. Falk makes the point that Christian attacks on evolution "do not simply represent minor disagreement with science on a peripheral issue. Rather [they] advocate a view that . . . the sciences of astronomy, astrophysics, nuclear physics, geology and biology are all fundamentally wrong. . . . So central are the notions of an old earth and the gradual appearance of life [that, were they wrong], the disciplines themselves would collapse."[9]

However, he wrote,

I expect that many persons in our churches will read this book and put it down still believing in sudden creation. From my perspective, that will be fine. . . . My prayer is that each person who reads it will come to an understanding that evangelical Christians need no longer feel that sudden creation is one of the canons (or for that matter, cannons!) of their faith. I hope that they will respect that one should be able to be accepted as an equal partner in Christ's body even if he or she believes that God created gradually.[10]

That is the burden of *Coming to Peace with Science*: "We do not all have to believe the same."[11] Falk urges, "Let us not ever allow the acid test of one's Christianity to become one's view of whether Adam and Eve are figurative alone or historical *and* figurative. It is the message itself, and belief that the message came from God, that is central."[12]

———————

While Falk insists that evangelical Christians may hold a variety of positions on origins, he is equally sure that positions condemning evolution can be toxic: "The church can get away with [antievolution] a little bit longer, but not much. It is going to hurt the church. Young people are not going to tolerate it."

He continues,

If a sizable segment of evangelical Christianity continues to tell its children the things that it has been telling them, a chasm is going to open up that will increasingly make Christianity inaccessible to individuals who believe that scientific investigation has revealed truth about the universe. . . . As our young people go to college and study, they will incorrectly perceive that they need to make a decision that is focused not so much on whether to pick up their cross and follow Jesus but on whether astronomy, astrophysics, nuclear physics, geology and biology are all very wrong.[13]

Falk notes his "hope that Christians will stop insisting that the sudden creation view be taught in the science classroom. If there is any lesson in this book, it is that the sudden creation view is not compatible with scientific data. It cannot be taught in a science classroom because it is not science. It is contrary to almost all of science. . . . It is something different, namely a particular view of Scripture. It is religion."[14]

The world-famous geneticist Francis Collins, head of the Human Genome Project, wrote a warm introduction to *Coming to Peace with Science* even though, at that point, the two men had never met. Eventually Collins would provide Falk with an avenue for advancing his views globally.

Following a stint in academic administration, Falk returned to the classroom. Interaction with students convinced him more than ever of the importance of the science-faith dialogue. These convictions got him invited to meet with a committee of the American Association for the Advancement of Science (AAAS) that aimed to promote understanding between scientists and evangelical Christians. As he prepared for the meeting, Falk decided to write Collins expressing his concerns, including his notes for interacting with the committee:

I go into this meeting with the following thoughts:

1. Mainstream evolutionary biology basically has it right, even though the tools used within the discipline cannot detect God's work within that process. Unfortunately the discipline has long been associated with statements in textbooks and by leading evolutionary biologists to the effect that evolutionary biology has excluded

supernatural activity from having participated in the origin or ongoing directions of life on earth. . . . The scientific enterprise has not carefully delimited the boundaries to which its methods can take the frontier of knowledge. . . .

2. Evangelical Christianity also basically has it right. . . . Humankind is innately self-centered and thereby alienated from God. The Bible records the story of God's ongoing effort to bring humankind to peace—peace with each other, peace with ourselves, and, pre-eminently, peace with our Maker. At the heart of evangelical Christianity is the story of the Creator taking on the form of a man in order that each of these facets of peace can be fully realized. As a result of this action humankind can be brought into personal relationship with its Maker. Unfortunately, there are many in evangelical Christianity who feel this story is irrevocably intertwined with a literal interpretation of the first three chapters of Genesis. Given the innate distrust of evangelicals for science (in part this is a result of science's spokespersons not respecting the boundaries of scientific knowledge as mentioned in #1, above), we are at a stalemate that will not soon go away. Since most evangelicals are not trained in science, it will be very, very difficult to help them understand just how solid the scientific evidence for evolutionary biology really is . . . even if the distrust could be removed.

3. In the meantime, evangelicals have become so good at indoctrinating their young (and not-so young) people with the importance of distrusting science, that there is a danger that the force of anti-science represented by this large group will come to significantly impact the scientific progress in our country. Many would say it already has.

4. . . . More and more young people who make the bold move of venturing out into the realm of science (many will be lured there by pre-med studies) will come to see that science basically has it right. Since their faith is so closely intertwined with an antiquated view of science, both will exit from these individuals' lives together. This will

be extremely unhealthy for evangelicalism as a movement, let alone for each individual for whom the loss of a life-enriching faith in a personal God may be gone forever.

5. The positions (science vs. anti-science) are very deeply entrenched within organizations, and we all know from Thomas Kuhn that paradigms don't shift by changing organizations . . . they shift through groundswells . . . most frequently by new blood . . . frequently young people with new ideas.

6. As a person who cares deeply about science, but even more deeply about faith in the living Christ, I believe there must be a paradigm shift. . . . I sense that AAAS would be able to free itself from some of the ideological baggage of some of its most vociferous spokespersons (e.g. Gould, Wilson et al.) and enter into an effort of this sort wholeheartedly. I am not so optimistic about large evangelical organizations. The forces of anti-scientism are so strong, that there are few that could work productively in a pro-science direction. . . .

7. I think that the leadership must come from within the AAAS and it must work with a core team of evangelicals. . . .

8. If there is not meaningful dialog and a prescribed course of action soon, we will continue towards a collision course some time in the coming decades from which neither side will emerge without deep wounds that will impact American society far too broadly.

If Falk's upbringing was narrow and enclosed, Collins's had been open to the extreme. His parents' freethinking rural home welcomed a wide variety of interesting folk attracted by a "happy mix of pastoral beauty, hard farm work, summer theater, and music." Musicians would crash at the farm for a few weeks before moving on; a young Bob Dylan was one among many who passed through with his guitar. It made an enchanted life for a homeschooled boy, but there was no God or Bible involved. Faith, so central to Falk's family, was unimportant to Collins's parents.

In college Collins became convinced that religious faith "held no foundational truth." He pursued chemistry and during PhD studies at Yale shifted from agnosticism to atheism—an aggressive sort of atheism that enjoyed embarrassing believers at the dinner table.

Growing increasingly interested in applying scientific learning to human problems, he went to medical school at the University of North Carolina in Chapel Hill before returning to Yale to do research in genetics.

Life as a medical doctor first caused Collins to doubt his atheism. Watching patients confront suffering and death, he was often struck by the role faith played. "If faith was a psychological crutch, I concluded, it must be a very powerful one," Collins wrote in *The Language of God*.[15] When one dying woman asked him what he believed, he was embarrassed to realize that he was not sure. He had never seriously studied the questions involved in faith.

He began to explore. A neighbor gave him a copy of C. S. Lewis's *Mere Christianity*, which impressed him with its powerful logic and opened his mind to further exploration. For two years he read and pondered.

His wife had begun attending a Methodist church and wanted him to join her, but Collins told her he didn't want to hear "about this Jesus junk." He wouldn't go to church, but he did eventually seek out his wife's pastor, Sam McMillan, and over a round of golf besieged him with questions.

On the eighteenth hole, McMillan had a moment of inspiration. As he told Peter Boyer in the *New Yorker*, "I grabbed the scorecard and wrote down, 'When God knocks on my door, in a way that I—not my wife or pastor, but I—know that it's God who's knocking on my door, I will then accept Jesus Christ.' I gave it to him. And he signed it."[16]

Months went by before McMillan heard from Collins again. He called from a hike in the Cascades, and shortly afterward he appeared at church saying he wanted to tell the congregation what had happened to him. On the hike he had encountered a vision of beauty, a frozen waterfall divided perfectly in three parts. It spoke to him of the Trinity. In the silent waterfall he heard God's knock. As he wrote in *The Language of God*, "Seeing no escape, I leapt."[17]

———

Though several years had passed since they had communicated over the introduction to Falk's book, Collins read Falk's notes for the upcoming meeting and asked to meet him for dinner when Falk was in Washington, DC. Subsequently, other meetings and seminars brought them closer together.

After publication of his best-selling book, *The Language of God*, which describes his journey of faith, Collins received so many e-mailed questions he determined to form a small organization to help answer them. As time went on, the mission of the organization, BioLogos, expanded. Funds were raised, mainly through a Templeton grant, to launch a website and other programs devoted to exploring science and faith questions from an evangelical perspective.

Ten days before BioLogos was to be introduced to the public, Collins was asked by President Obama to head the National Institutes of Health. Since the government would not allow him to hold this powerful role— possibly the most influential position in the world of science—while running another organization, Collins had to suddenly resign from BioLogos. Falk, already involved, took over as president. Under his lead, it has emerged as an important group for Christians advocating *evolutionary creation*. (The term puts creation at the center, modified by evolution, the reverse of the situation with the older term *theistic evolution*.)

In this role Falk has stuck to his plea for Christians to love and respect each other. For example, BioLogos invited Southern Baptist biblical scholars to publish essays critical of the BioLogos perspective on the BioLogos website in order to foster mutual understanding. Falk has been encouraged by the interactions and hopes they will lead to further face-to-face discussions.

"We must be patient with each other and allow each other to follow truth as we see it in Scripture," Falk wrote. "We must recognize that we will never reach the point where we all see Scripture the same way. . . . We are one body and we must nurture and care for each other, all the more so when we think differently on some points. . . . When there is division in the church, it will be difficult for the thirsty to find their way to Jesus."[18]

For himself, Falk rejoices in the sense that he has, after a lifelong search, come to a full understanding of how God has done his work in gradual creation. In *Coming to Peace with Science* he was vague, speaking of God as an artist or an orchestra leader. His great "aha" moment came more recently with the help of a young Oxford physicist, Ard Louis. "Ard said, 'If you take God out of the equation, not only does nothing work, but creation doesn't exist. God's spirit is always active in upholding creation. The laws we have discovered are simply describing how God works, his ongoing activity.' That helped me so much.

"Theistic evolution might have left it there," saying that God created through ordinary physical processes. But Louis also helped Falk to see that other things were possible. Nothing in science rules out the miraculous. "We need not say that God was intervening miraculously or nonregularly, but he might have been. In ways we can never really measure he might have stepped in at the Cambrian explosion or at the origin of life. As scientists we can't sort that out. Miracles of that sort are not discernible by science." Falk doesn't think the Bible requires us to see miracles at every point where new species are created. He leaves room for creative disagreement on how that happened.

With that fuller sense of God's presence and power in the ordinary processes of life, and the possibility of miraculous processes, Falk feels that his lifelong quest for understanding has been answered. "This now makes sense, consistent with biblical faith and with life as a scientist."

Asked whether the evolutionary mechanism of mutation and selection can explain biological innovation, he says, "We don't have the full explanation. Mainstream science will tell you that we don't know the limits of mutation and selection. That's what makes evolutionary biology so fascinating: figuring it out."

9 Ard Louis
Evangelical Science

Ard Louis (pronounced Looey) grew up in the West African country of Gabon. At a small Christian and Missionary Alliance mission station, Bongolo, his parents taught biology in a school run by the Gabonese church. Set deep in the rain forest, the school was designed to provide a high school education to local villagers.

Bongolo had a vibrant church, the school, a dispensary, and little else. To buy the most rudimentary supplies, one drove half a day. Louis ran wild and barefoot in the jungle, climbing trees, eating wild fruit, hunting small animals, and building forts. "We did crazy things," he says with a fond smile. "I would never let my children do such things." A bottle-raised pet chimpanzee, bought for its weight in sardines after hunters killed its mother, was a regular companion.

His parents were "Dutch hippies," Louis says, who came to Gabon not long after their conversion to a newly emerging charismatic Dutch

Christianity. Neither parent had a Christian background; Louis's mother had been president of the Nietzsche Society and came from a long line of staunch atheists. As a student Louis's skeptic father got kicked out of his housing for some misdemeanor. Desperate for a room, he interviewed with a strange, ardent Christian man who inquired about the state of his soul. To get the room, Louis's father pretended to pray for salvation, then later roared with laughter when he recounted the story to friends. The landlord was a taxidermist with a vast collection of rare stuffed animals in his basement that he expected to come back to life when Christ returned. He believed that, praying, one had to hold hands in a certain way lest the blessing slip off them.

Having tricked him with a prayer, Louis's father felt obliged to play along with the man's religion. At some point it occurred to him that, odd as the man's ideas were, they were tremendously important if true. He thought that as an academic, he ought to investigate for himself. Eventually, another man, a doctor, helped him to genuine faith.

"Thus I've always had a soft spot for crazy Christians," Louis says. "I'm very thankful to that man. My life would have been very different without him."

When Louis was eight his family moved into Libreville, Gabon's capital. There his father worked as a botanist for the government and university, collecting and cataloging the vast variety of plant life in the Gabonese rain forest. Louis continued to go to school in Bongolo, now as a boarder.

Louis was taught the basics of young earth creationism through his school, populated by the children of American missionaries. A book, *The Handy Dandy Evolution Refuter*, provided intellectual fuel. "My parents always thought the Americans were odd. Whenever I came home with creationist stuff, they never said it was wrong. They said, 'Take it with a grain of salt.'" As botanists, they studied plant life as it existed, not as it had come to be. Evolution was not a major issue for them. It certainly wasn't for Louis because he had zero interest in biology. At the beginning levels, biology involved much memorization of facts. Louis was far more interested in the fluid, abstract world of physics and mathematics.

As he grew older, Louis began to think for himself in the area of faith. In his family's Gabonese church, life in the spirit was rich and expressive. Many of Louis's Gabonese friends told stories of supernatural experiences, including healing. Louis says he came to faith "seeing the dynamic power of the gospel in the lives of my African friends, transforming their lives."

The Conservative Baptist boarding school that Louis attended in Ivory Coast, beginning when he was fourteen, took a much less expansive view toward the gifts of the Spirit. They believed and taught that supernatural gifts had ended in the time of the apostles. Louis began to read the Bible for himself and, for the first time, question who was right. He could see no reason why healing and prophecy and speaking in tongues—gifts he saw in the New Testament—should not continue.

About that time a friend at school suddenly found himself praying in another language. He had no idea what had happened to him until his Assemblies of God roommate explained to him that he had spoken in tongues. Word spread quickly, and a small group of students, including Louis, grew excited. In response, an alarmed school administration decided to ban them from meeting together.

"If you are fifteen," Louis says, "what is more exciting than being banned?" Sometimes they sneaked out of the dorm to surreptitiously pray for sick staff members who had requested their prayers.

"I remember one girl who had a very severe back injury. She was in traction and about to be airlifted back home to the United States. Before she left, one of my friends prayed for her to be healed. She instantly jumped up and started running around. Though I found this incredible, I did recognize that this girl's experience of prayer and healing matched exactly what I had read in Bible."[1]

On another occasion Louis was sick with the early stages of malaria. He called two of his friends to pray for him and within moments felt completely recovered. "I was sincerely shocked." Thinking that he might be imagining the change, he went to a dorm wall where he had often jumped to see how high he could touch. Now, he jumped and touched higher than he had ever done before.

"These healings were an important experience for me. I first came to believe [in God's power to heal] based on Scripture. It was an experiment. Come up with a theory, try it out, and then it works. It gave me a lot of trust in Scripture. When you are that age you have to find the faith on your own."

As he probed more deeply into the Bible, he discovered that not every issue could be decided so straightforwardly. Some things, such as predestination and free will, did not seem to add up. During his last year of high school, Louis taught himself the rudiments of quantum mechanics. In that mathematical theory he saw for himself that an electron can be described as a particle and, equally truly, as a wave. The mathematics is precise, but the human mind cannot reflect that precision except through the analogy of particle and wave. "This led me to suspect that when I encountered what seemed to be profound logical or theological mysteries, a radically different way of interpreting the problem could make the whole thing come together in a very powerful way. Just as C. S. Lewis wrote about a 'deeper magic' in his Narnia series, there could perhaps also be a 'deeper logic.'"[2]

At the age of seventeen, Louis left Africa, returning to Holland for university. He went alone, to stay with a family while he completed Dutch high school and then matriculated at Utrecht University. It was bewildering to enter the speed and intensity of Dutch life, let alone adjust to technologies Louis had never used—such as the train and the telephone.

"If you have never taken a train before, it's very confusing. You don't know where it's going to stop. I remember the first time I went to my uncle's house. I had to phone him when I arrived. I went to a phone booth, but I had never used one before. When I tried to make the call, it wasn't working. I look around and see a Moroccan man. 'Can you help me?' I asked, and he came over to look at what I was doing. 'That's an area code,' he said. I said, 'What's an area code?' I turned away for a moment, and when I turned back he was running up the platform. He thought I was up to something.

"The difficulty is that you are a hidden immigrant. You look and sound like anybody else. You could tell by people's body language that you had done something wrong, but you didn't know what. I would purposely make a mistake with my Dutch. They would hear that and say, 'Where are you from? Oh, Africa!' and everybody would visibly relax. Otherwise they think you are a crazy person."

The pleasurable part of returning to Holland, a home he had never known, was the intellectual challenge. For the first time, his classes were hard. But the pleasurable academic rigor of university physics also challenged his faith because the atmosphere was so unrelentingly anti-Christian. "It had a slow-drip effect on my confidence. It probably was not so much the science itself as the university way of looking at the world. The great men and women of the university don't believe in God. Therefore if you believe in God, something is wrong with you. I thought a smart person couldn't be a Christian. It sounds really naive, but it had a big impact on me.

"I was lucky. There was one Christian professor in physics, a brilliant lecturer. I went to his lectures in quantum mechanics my second year, and they were fantastic. Then I went to his home and found out he was a real Christian." That one counterexample was enough to help carry Louis through with his faith intact.

A different kind of challenge emerged during his PhD studies at Cornell University in Ithaca, New York. "I hadn't really thought too much about science and religion. I was quite happy to compartmentalize. I thought of science as a fun thing to do. I loved it. I also thought of it as a means to an end, for getting a job. Maybe I could be a missionary in a closed country by getting a job as a scientist. Maybe this was a way I could reach my colleagues for Christ.

"At Cornell I began to read theologians who pointed out that being a Christian means that your work has value intrinsically. For God it is not a means to an end but a means of worship. If God called me to science, I would serve God by being the best scientist I could be. Interestingly, American thinkers like Mark Noll helped me see this, although they were building on Dutch Reformed thinkers that I somehow had not seen. I had Americans point out to me my own Dutch heritage."

While his understanding of science and faith was expanding, so was his sense of ministry. Cornell's Christian students had a long-standing group, related to the national organization InterVarsity Christian Fellowship. The year Louis arrived, a separate group of graduate students split off to meet independently.

Louis joined in with them enthusiastically but noticed that the group was almost entirely Anglo, whereas the grad student population came from all over the world. He proposed and launched an international fellowship, which grew rapidly and became something of a model for InterVarsity grad groups across the country. Louis was invited to offer a seminar at Urbana, a large triennial student conference, to explain how the international fellowship had been launched. It would prove to be a pivotal event for him.

Louis thought that since Urbana was paying his expenses to come, he might offer a second seminar in the bargain. He decided to talk about science and faith partly because of his sense that he had a lot to think through. Reading widely in preparation, he came to the conclusion that an underlying issue controlled all controversies: how to obtain reliable knowledge about the world. He talked, therefore, about what science could and could not accomplish.

The common assumption that science was the arbiter of all truth was based, he told the Urbana seminar, on a confusion of mechanism and meaning. He cited the famous example of someone noticing a kettle on the stove and asking why the water was boiling. "'There is a heat source transmitting thermal energy across the container wall into the fluid, and that's increasing the average mean square velocity of the molecules, which is proportional to the temperature. Once that temperature reaches one hundred degrees centigrade, there's a collective phase transition from a condensed phase to an expanded phase, which we call boiling.' That's all true. That's a mechanistic explanation. 'Why is the water boiling?' 'I'm making a cup of tea. Would you like one?' That's also an explanation. Just because I've given you the mechanistic explanation doesn't mean that I have explained away all other forms of meaning."

Louis believed that many controversies were based on this confusion of mechanism and meaning. Antireligious scientists like Richard Dawkins claimed that an evolutionary mechanism explained everything. Ironically, some of Dawkins's Christian opponents accepted his premise. "They think that God works in the gaps of our knowledge, that God is glorified by what we don't understand. So if someone says we don't understand this thing, we are going to get very happy because there in the gap is God." Louis made the basic point that one might explain exactly how a process works, mechanically speaking, yet say nothing about what was behind it. God's presence is understood at another level.

Louis's Urbana talk on science and faith proved to be quite influential, convincing a number of students to carry on with a career in science. It led to more invitations to talk and a growing sense that there was a ministry in helping people understand science and faith better. Louis is convinced that the antiscience reputation of evangelical Christians keeps many people away from faith. "Being very pragmatic, if I only cared about evangelism, I would still care about these things. The long-term impact on the evangelical church is going to be really dire."

When he finished his PhD at Cornell, Louis wanted to go where he could make a difference in people's lives. That was a major reason for taking a job at Cambridge University in England—it was closer to Holland and other European countries. Louis saw that Christian fellowships at major US universities had dozens of full-time staff. European universities had few, if any.

On moving to Cambridge, Louis chose to work in an area of physics that many regarded as a dubious road to success. Physics had traditionally focused on the behavior of single objects. Louis wanted to study the unorchestrated interaction of millions of tiny objects. He and his colleagues initiated new ways of understanding these interactions using statistical methods and quantum calculations.

The uncanny and little-understood mechanisms of the cell stood out as problems to be understood in such systematic ways. The parts assembled themselves out of thousands of different proteins. The more biologists learned of these tiny factories, the more astonishing and mysterious their processes seemed. "Physicists like myself think there are going to be new principles of emergent behavior that we are going to have to understand." For the first time in his life, Louis began to find biology interesting.

Teaching at Cambridge and later at Oxford, Louis put together an interdisciplinary research group. They concentrated on the simplest biological system they could experiment with, a virus. Louis immersed himself in the problems that biochemists face and gradually learned the way biologists think.

When he attended a meeting of the European Leadership Forum, a Christian conference, he followed a science track dominated by intelligent design proponents. ID was new to Louis. Its basic appeal interested him—the idea that you can tell, in a systematic and scientific way, whether something is created by an intelligent, planned process or by brute, random forces. As for the presentations, he was less impressed. "As a scientist I could tell these were secondhand arguments. The people were not really on top of the science. I thought, *I need to learn. I need to read all the ID literature.* That's when I got really interested in evolution."

He found two kinds of arguments in the ID literature. One he agreed with completely: Phillip Johnson's contention that evolution sometimes functions as a proto-religion. Another was the claim associated with William Dembski and Michael Behe that logic and mathematics prove that evolution is incapable of producing what Dembski calls *specified complexity.*

That fits right into Louis's area of expertise. "When I first heard Dembski's claim, I thought, *That can't be right. There's no way that can be right. And if someone claims to [have proved] that, either he's a supreme genius, the greatest of our time, or he's a crank.*"

Louis explains why few scientists take Dembski seriously: "[As an Oxford professor] I get e-mails all the time from people who claim to have disproved quantum mechanics. I could spend my life trying to figure out what they did wrong. It's a waste of time." If Dembski could really prove that evolution was impossible using only logic and mathematics, then that would be the most stunning proof of the century, from Louis's perspective.

Amazing proofs generally come from scientists with an impressive record, however. The fact that Dembski has no track record of accomplishment in science makes scientists inherently skeptical. "Physical scientists might [listen to it with interest] but then say, 'Who are you? Publish it somewhere [in a peer-reviewed journal] and maybe we'll take you seriously.' The system isn't always fair, but that's how it works." Nobody at the top of the field is willing to give the time to closely examine a claim from someone with no reputation.

More interesting to Louis is what ID reveals about the difference between the physical sciences and the biological. "I've had numerous discussions with physical scientists who really like these information theory arguments. They think they are very strong. Unless they start working in biology, it's hard for them to understand why biologists don't take it seriously."

As a physicist, Louis finds himself in a very different world when he interacts with biologists. Their experiments seem messy and the data often not clean. And yet biology has a track record of tremendous success. To work alongside biologists Louis has had to learn how they think.

"Even though they don't do it the way I would, I've learned that they do have pretty good instincts for what they can trust and what they can't. It's just they are looser with data than a physicist might be. They have to be because they are looking at really difficult problems. You have to go on, even though you aren't sure where it all leads."

Biologists do not pursue systematic understanding in the way physicists do, Louis says. They tend to focus on case-by-case investigations into how things work. Life is so supremely complex that top-down systematic understanding is improbable. No matter how much you know, surprises are always just around the corner. Just when you think you understand a biological system, it reacts in a completely unexpected way.

That helps explain why ID, which operates from a top-down, logical point of view, gets no traction with biologists. "From a biologist's perspective, the only way you can show that no biological mechanism could generate complexity is by looking at all the mechanisms that are and showing that they wouldn't work. But we don't know what all the mechanisms are. So the best thing we can do is just look and keep on looking. Given that biologists can't do that kind of abstract, theoretical stuff [the way that physicists do], it's just a nonquestion to them. Dembski says, 'They're ignoring me. They're biased.' They aren't biased. You're just not communicating in a language they can use. They are suspicious of abstract arguments that aren't based in experiments."

At a more fundamental level, Louis sees a naive evidentialism motivating atheist scientists like Dawkins and many of their Christian opponents. The presupposition, he says, is that God should be visibly provable in roughly the same way that you would prove the existence of a flying teapot. "You have smuggled in a lot of assumptions about God, that God must be something out there who pokes the universe occasionally, and if you don't see him poking the universe, then he must not exist."

A God who creates and sustains the universe, who is immanent in all things seen and unseen, may not be subject to that kind of evidence. Certainly, "nobody can look at the exquisite beauty of the world without thinking that it does seem to point to an intelligent agent behind it. And I don't see how showing that the mechanism of evolution could or could not produce a bacterial flagellum motor does a lot to that. It's still a beautiful world.

"I use an analogy in my talks. If I give you a fully formed LEGO train, that's cool. If I give you a box of LEGOs and I shake the box, and out comes a fully formed LEGO train, that's even cooler. That's what the evolutionary argument is: this is a world that can make itself. I think that's unbelievably cool. I can look at that and think, *That's amazing.* If I go to a mountain and see the grandeur of the world, or I go diving in the sea and see the beauty there, all those things speak to me of the glory and grandeur of God. I don't see where the ID argument adds to that. In fact it subtracts from it because it seems that the really key point is in these little niggly bits you are looking at."

———————

To look at him, one might mistake Louis for a cheerful undergraduate, with his youthful, pixieish face and friendly manner. When he talks, his excitement often overplays his tongue so that words come out herky-jerky, with multiple false starts. Gravitas is lacking, especially considering he is a Reader at Oxford University, equivalent to a tenured professor at one of the oldest and grandest universities in the world.

Louis wears his intellect lightly, which reflects not only his casual style but also his fundamental perspective on the limits on intellectual inquiry. He is an active member of the prayer team at Oxford's St. Aldates Church, a historic Anglican congregation that is part of the British charismatic renewal. Louis believes that the prayer team provides essential balance to his work as a scientist. "When someone says, I am sick, my intellect doesn't help them. I have to pray for them and ask God to help. How well you pray or hear God's voice doesn't correlate with intellect. It keeps my feet on the ground.

"In my work, we have a very particular way of looking at the world, a very powerful way we call *methodological naturalism*. As a Christian I can make a good argument for it. It would be odd if there were miracles in my lab or in my calculations. What I am studying are the regular ways God sustains the world. If there is a God who is faithful, then I expect his rules to be trustworthy and regular, and if God is intelligent, I might even need to understand his rules.

"I think Western cessationism comes from people acting like that all day long, and they think that's the way it is. But I don't think that's the way it is. If you read the Bible, that's not the way it was. It's particularly important for me as a scientist to be involved in something like praying for the sick because that does act on a different plane."

Louis believes that pentecostal and charismatic Christians have a particular contribution to make to the discussion of evolution. "The evolution-creation debate gets tense because there is a fear of knocking down the foundations of faith. This is the way creationists argue, that the whole thing will collapse if you mess with your interpretation of Genesis. I don't find that so worrying. Charismatics find it easier to explore different ideas. They take the Bible very seriously, but they know that God is real."

The most difficult issue, Louis believes, lies not in the science or in the biblical interpretation but in "how do we as a church decide these things? Like the guy I had in my office [an Oxford graduate student]. He says, 'What about Wells, Behe? They are scientists. Who should I believe?' He can't tell. Just because the academic community says something doesn't mean it's true. They have been wrong before. It's good to have some skepticism.

"The real problem is that the church doesn't have a place for evangelical scholars to devote their lives to a very complicated subject, think about it, test it with other scholars, and eventually come to some kind of consensus. Something as complicated as evolution has scientific, biblical, historical, theological, and philosophical dimensions. No one person is going to be smart enough to solve all those things for the church. It has to be a communal thing.

"Fundamentally, there is something deeply odd when a country thinks that a rural judge in Pennsylvania without a science background is going to be able to decide whether ID is science." And, Louis points out, it's not much better for Christians. "If you are a Christian interested in this question, you have no idea who you can trust. It comes down to individuals. Maybe you decide you can trust Francis Collins because he seems to be very smart. Or you trust Stephen Meyer [an ID advocate] because he seems very smart and godly.

"We know from experience that it takes a long time to decide things. You can be wrong for a long time. So there needs to be a place where people can devote their lives to these things and work in community.

"We can fool ourselves. We can be wrong. There's something deeply Christian about the idea that we need communities who help each other because our intellect is fallen, and we can be mistaken. One of the difficulties in the evangelical church is there aren't such communities.

"I don't want to knock the importance of lay understanding. Certainly, somebody from a charismatic background believes that you can have real insight from God. But evolution is the kind of thing that is discerned by a community over a long period of time." Louis, a brilliant mind in many dimensions, humbly hopes for that kind of community discernment.

10 Denis Alexander
Speaking the Scientist's Language

From one view Cambridge, England, appears to be a very beautiful Merry Olde England theme park. Ancient creamy stone buildings back up on the River Cam, where tourists in small boats punt up and down by vast stretches of green lawn. One easily forgets that this is a working city, full of classrooms and laboratories.

Cambridge is where Denis Alexander, a tall, trim man with a shock of silver hair, leads the Faraday Institute, based at St. Edmund's College. He founded it in 2006 after a lifetime of academic research in biochemistry.

Faraday exists to communicate a Christian perspective on science to scientists. The program has the look and feel of a graduate seminar, taking up such topics as "human genomics and the image of God."

This makes Alexander sound rather stuffy. In reality he is a Clark Kent figure. His career has been marked by adventure—artillery fire and death threats—and an eagerness to (cheerfully) witness to his faith under strikingly difficult conditions.

————

Alexander grew up in a distinguished family just outside London. His mother was one of the first women at Oxford to study physiology, a subject she later taught. His father was a timber merchant. Both parents had deep roots in a very strict group of Brethren, a small, influential denomination with a reputation for serious Bible study. When Alexander was seven, their group veered toward a ferocious separatism associated with a dictatorial New Yorker named Big Jim Taylor. Taylor began to send out edicts telling the members what they could wear and with whom they could associate. Alarmed by this extremism, Alexander's parents decided to leave. It was a traumatic shift, but for Alexander it was "a wonderful liberation." The family joined a group of Open Brethren, where life was much less supervised. He was allowed to join an interdenominational youth group known as the Crusaders. It fit with the family style. Alexander remembers "very tolerant" parents who let him run free.

Still, church was at the center of everything, especially on Sundays when he usually attended three different meetings wearing uncomfortable suits. Brethren do not have ordained clergy, so many laypeople contribute to teaching in their assemblies. During Alexander's adolescent years, his family's small fellowship included three full professors from London University. Growing up in this high-powered academic environment, Alexander never lacked intellectual confidence.

Nor did he lack intellectual challenge. His private high school had a chaplain of a liberal Christian persuasion. The "public school religion" he "force-fed" the boys was very unfavorable to evangelicals. Alexander prayed for the chaplain's conversion and organized a panel discussion to give a different perspective. Bypassing the chaplain's authority, he invited four well-regarded professors to talk about their faith. He even invited other schools to attend, and buses carrying hundreds of students showed up. Only at the last moment did it occur to Alexander to inform the chaplain of the program.

This same confidence made Alexander a writer. He loved composing persuasive essays and won several prizes. When he was fifteen Alexander saw a magazine advertisement for the School of Successful Writing. The ad promised you would earn back the expense of the course, or they would refund it. Given that the cost of enrolling was high, this was an enticing guarantee. The correspondence course taught would-be writers how to study publications to learn what kinds of articles they were likely to buy. Alexander hit the jackpot with his very first effort, an account of a trip across a glacier in Switzerland. He received a check from the *Lady*, a well-known women's magazine, and never looked back.

He wanted to write about bigger subjects. He dreamed of writing that would tell the story of Christian faith with devastating effectiveness.

In school Alexander hated mathematics, but he loved biology. "I liked knowing how things connect up. I was never good on isolated facts. I'm hopeless at crossword puzzles. I liked the big story." For biology, evolution was the big story, and nothing in Alexander's conservative Christian fellowship disputed it. Very few young earth creationists lived in England; unlike Americans, Britons had painlessly accepted evolution as the way God had created. Alexander never met a creationist at Oxford, he says. His first and only encounter was with a Frenchman he was paired up with one summer for door-to-door evangelism in Paris.

As he prepared for college he thought seriously about studying history—the big story, again—like his famous historian uncle, A. J. P. Taylor, who could be seen on TV giving lectures. Or perhaps he might study medicine, like his mother and a grandfather whose microscope he inherited. His mother thought science would be the most flexible choice, and he ultimately agreed. He was accepted into Oxford University to study biochemistry.

———————

Students in the UK typically have a gap year before they begin university, a year that they fill with travel or volunteer service. Alexander considered going to Africa to work in a hospital. When that didn't materialize, he took up an offer from an uncle who was general manager of Schweppes, the beverage company. Instead of going to Africa, Alexander took his first-ever plane flight to Canada, where he worked in a Welch's Grape Juice factory in Ontario. Workers were allowed to drink all the grape juice they liked, a privilege that soon paled.

At a Brethren Assembly in St. Catharines, Ontario, he met some young Christians planning a summer evangelism outreach in Quebec. They invited him to join and to attend a meeting in Chicago for Operation Mobilisation (OM), the organization behind the outreach. OM was only a few years old, led by a young, charismatic George Verwer. Listening to Verwer in Chicago, Alexander was deeply challenged. This was commitment of a kind he had never encountered, a sold-out sacrificial discipleship to match the radicalism of the 1960s. For OMers, evangelism was the only cause, and giving up everything to serve was the only lifestyle. Alexander felt a very clear, strong missionary call and over-powering guilt for the thoughtless way he had bought an expensive train ticket to cross North America and back.

When he asked for advice about this extravagance, cooler heads prevailed. He was encouraged to go on his trip and enjoy it. He did, and while in Colorado he hiked for several days in the mountains, seeing more bears than people. During that lonely journey his calling solidified. Some words of Jesus struck him powerfully: "To whom much is given, much will be required." He knew that with his background and family, he had been given tremendous assets. He could not give less. He believed he must ultimately leave England to serve God in places of great need.

Beginning his studies at Oxford he launched himself into Christian Union (CU) activities—he would eventually become president of this venerable evangelical fellowship—and began trying to radicalize it. Organizing a visit by Verwer, he succeeded in recruiting many students to go with OM on summer missions in Europe. The ethos of OM was difficult for the "wise and balanced ways of the CU" to absorb, but thanks in part to Alexander, it became an accepted part of evangelical faith at Oxford. "That radical movement had great traction because it was a time of huge social change and upheaval." Throughout his years at Oxford, Alexander spent every summer with OM, a commitment that sustained his calling to serve God overseas. "I think unless people are a little bit radical at that age they'll probably be stone dead by the age of sixty."

———————

At Oxford every undergraduate is assigned a tutor, a younger faculty member who meets weekly to guide his studies. Alexander's was a young biochemist named Arthur Peacocke, known for his studies of thermodynamics and the structure of DNA. Alexander remembers Peacocke as a difficult tutor, "arriving in a whirl of papers and departing in a cloud of dust for the next appointment."[1] Peacocke's background was in physics, and his mind was far more mathematical than Alexander could appreciate.

Peacocke was developing a stronger interest in faith, however, and launched a discussion group that Alexander joined eagerly. The group began a chapter-by-chapter reading of J. S. Whale's *Christian Doctrine*, an orthodox Christian book from which Alexander says he learned a good deal of theology. As most of the members of the group were in science, they worked through the intersection of Christian doctrine with science—formative discussions for a young undergraduate who was interested in how things connect to a big story.

Unknown to Alexander, Peacocke soon began writing his first book on the connections between faith and science, a subject for which ultimately he would become very well known. Unknown to Peacocke, Alexander began writing *his* first book in the same area. Alexander remembers discussing this with Peacocke years later. "He said, 'I really enjoyed reading your little book.'" Alexander laughs at the adjective. "The tutor-student relationship never really changes."

Peacocke was far more liberal in his theology than Alexander, but nevertheless, looking back, Alexander recognizes how much he took on board from Peacocke's thinking. His emphasis on the immanence of God in creation would become particularly important as Alexander tried to understand God's role in creation through evolution.

Alexander feels he was more influenced by a visiting speaker, Donald MacKay. An influential neuroscientist, MacKay was an incisive and outspoken Christian who could and did debate figures like B. F. Skinner. He published in both *Nature* and *Mind,* an important journal in philosophy—a remarkable cross disciplinary feat. MacKay's writings about free will and determinism, as well as the complementarity between religion and science, were fundamental building blocks for Alexander's understanding. Even more, MacKay was a model of the kind of man he wanted to be: impeccably scholarly, courageous, and persuasive in his Christian witness.

Early in his time at Oxford, Alexander heard an OM leader speak about Turkey, a country where a Christian church barely existed and where missionaries could not operate. The only way to reach Turkey was while holding jobs that were useful to the country. That clicked with Alexander—both the need and the way of going. After his second year at university, he hitchhiked to Istanbul to attend a Turkish language school. The visit confirmed his calling: Turkey was his destiny.

As he neared graduation, therefore, he began to write to universities and colleges in Turkey, looking for a teaching position. None came forward. Several wrote back to say that he would need a PhD.

Alexander did not want to work toward a PhD. He was tired of school. He felt that life was too urgent for more time in the laboratory. "People are dying without Christ!"

Despondent, he sought counsel from one of the London University professors in his Brethren fellowship, an Assyriologist named Donald Wiseman. Wiseman was sympathetic. "I understand how you feel," he said. He hadn't wanted to do a PhD either; he had felt the work wasn't spiritual. Nevertheless he reassured Alexander, "If you go and do your PhD, it won't seem very long."

———

Alexander did his PhD in brain biochemistry at the Institute of Psychiatry in London. Considering how eager he was to get the degree done, he was fortunate to be assigned a topic that proved easy. It took him only two years to work out how the sodium-potassium pump functions at the biochemical level in neural cells, plus a few more months to write it up. He conducted the research using ox brains; Alexander procured them at a Jewish slaughterhouse (because kosher practice meant the oxen had their throats slit, with their brains left undamaged) and carried them, frozen in dry ice, to the laboratory on his 49cc Honda motorbike. During the same period he met the woman who would become his wife. The two of them had many adventures riding together on the Honda through the streets of London.

"The general attitude toward religion in the Institute of Psychiatry at that time can best be described as 'frosty,'" Alexander writes. "Religious beliefs were generally equated with some kind of obsessional neurosis, possibly to be patronized, but certainly not to be taken seriously as claims to reality."[2] Freud's reductionist view of religion had permeated many minds.

This was a different challenge from the one he had typically encountered at Oxford. There, Christianity was challenged as old-fashioned, out of touch, bourgeois, and conservative. For most Oxford students, Christian faith was part of the Establishment. In the era of sexual liberation and protests against the Vietnam War, it seemed outdated and irrelevant. The challenge for Christians was to establish that genuine

Christianity was not, in fact, part of the Establishment but a radical challenge to all, Establishment or not.

The reductionistic attitude of the psychiatrists would become the chief challenge of coming generations. It was difficult to break through the prevalent attitudes and have an intelligent discussion. Alexander recognized the need for Christians in science to present their faith in a thoughtful and compelling way. There were at the time almost no such books available. Alexander, at twenty-five, finished up his PhD and set out to write one.

His older brother David had recently started Lion Publishing. He commissioned Denis to write and (typical older brother, Alexander says) gave him an outline of what to say. In a matter of months Alexander produced *Beyond Science*, which made a significant splash. Though it aimed at a popular audience, it was not a simplistic book. Written with skeptical psychiatrists in mind, it showed the intelligence and the up-to-date scientific knowledge that a PhD biochemist with an Oxford degree would be expected to have. It fully respected science while pointing out that science had limitations in what it could say and in how it could help. It made an appeal for genuine Christian faith, as opposed to the Establishment church that had begun in the Roman Empire as an accommodation to political power.

Today Alexander shudders to think of his bravado. Nevertheless, "I still come across people today who say how useful they found it in developing their own thinking: that science and faith were friends not foes, and that scientific advances were throwing up a host of questions that science itself was quite unable to address, but for which Christian faith had the answers."[3]

————

His book completed, his PhD completed, his marriage celebrated, Alexander waited for news from Turkey. He had been promised a position at a university in Ankara, but written confirmation did not come. Eventually, tired of waiting, he and his bride loaded up a van and drove to Turkey. The journey took them a week. When they arrived in Ankara, they discovered there was no job after all. Another position was unexpectedly available at another university, however, and he took it. This would become a lifelong pattern. Something always turned up. The Alexanders settled into academic work, adjusting to life in Turkey long before the country had become a tourist destination.

Left-wing factions dominated the university. "The Maoists fought the Trotskyites, and the Trotskyites fought the Marxist-Leninists. Actually, half the time I don't think even the students really knew who was fighting whom." Alexander was not threatened personally. Though the students would endlessly chant, "Death to America," they were quite friendly when they came in for their biochemistry lectures. As time went on, though, the battles between factions became more fraught. They were fought with real guns. Alexander was thankful for the large desk in his office, behind which he would hide when bullets were flying.

The Alexanders welcomed to their home the few Christians they met, and a small church began to meet there regularly. Since Turkey was officially secular, their action was perfectly legal, but eventually, it became a problem for the government. The economy deteriorated badly. Street battles escalated until the country was close to civil war. People died by the scores on a daily basis. In such an environment the civil authorities were hypersensitive. In 1979 the Alexanders went to see about having their visas renewed and were told they had thirty days to leave the country. One of Alexander's uncles was British foreign secretary Tony Crosland. Alexander dropped his name shamelessly, managing to win multiple delays.

It was never clear just what they had done to set off alarms. On one of his many visits to a government office, Alexander was treated to a view of his security file. It was staggeringly voluminous. Judging strictly by its size, it was obvious they had been closely watched and reported on.

Ultimately, the security forces told the university authorities not to renew Alexander's job contract, and the Alexanders had to leave. They departed just before a military coup.

———————

By that time the Alexanders had three small children. Returning to England after nine years in Turkey, they might well have found it appropriate to settle into a more conventional lifestyle. But when a job offer came from the American University in Beirut to set up a biochemical genetics laboratory, there was little hesitation. God had called them to serve overseas. The call had not changed.

The main catch was that Alexander had no formal training in genetic diseases or the techniques he would be using in a genetics laboratory. He had to retrain, taking two months in a London hospital before moving to Beirut.

Lebanon was a very different scene, although just as dicey. The country had not recovered from civil war just five years earlier. Beirut was governed, somewhat, by a collection of militias, of whom the most powerful was the Palestine Liberation Organization (PLO). As in Ankara, the Alexanders experienced intermittent warfare, this time with artillery. The university hospital where Alexander set up his lab was in the heart of the city, where shells often fell. Occasionally, the staff had to move experiments away from windows and into a corridor, where they would be shielded from shrapnel and other ordnance.

Alexander's work joined people of every faction and faith. They worked respectfully and appreciatively together. And their work in detecting genetic disease was particularly relevant in a country where many ethnic groups married first cousins and therefore experienced very high levels of genetic abnormalities. Some families lost children repeatedly to the same genetic disease. There were terrible ethical dilemmas to sort out, since the only real treatment for these awful diseases was abortion.

Meanwhile the political situation steadily worsened. Twice the Alexanders were evacuated, only to return to Beirut when the situation stabilized. Finally, when American bombers took off from England to bomb Libya, trying to kill dictator Muammar Qaddafi, the situation became fundamentally unsafe. Three Western hostages were killed in Beirut as retaliation. One was the director of the language school where Alexander's wife taught. "Our Lebanese friends said, 'We love you—please leave now!' We left within forty-eight hours with experiments sitting unfinished on the lab bench and children wailing as they said farewell to the family cats."[4]

So began, inauspiciously, Alexander's reintroduction to Great Britain and to the science and faith dialogue he had mainly left behind during his fifteen years in the Middle East. "Reentry into British life proved more problematic than readjusting to British tea (with milk—ugh!) and the terrible weather. A life of research in the UK had never been on my agenda. Fortunately, I had never left active scientific research and teaching and had managed to get a few papers published in decent genetics journals whilst in Beirut. Fortunately, also, no one had told me that getting one's first job in academic science in Britain at the age of forty-one is impossible."

Alexander says he didn't worry much. He has always been an optimist and never doubted that something good would turn up. It did. A one-year job turned into three years, which led to another job, which led eventually to his becoming chair of the Molecular Immunology Programme at the Babraham Institute in Cambridge. It was a time when the British economy was booming, and money flowed into basic research. After spending years borrowing and scrounging in order to do basic experiments, Alexander found that he could have any equipment or supplies he wanted. He had to retrain, again, in an entirely new field, but he made the transformation successfully.

Britain had changed. Instead of the politicized atmosphere of the 1960s, in which faith had to show its relevance to society, Britons seemed to have withdrawn into more private worlds. They thought most of their careers, not politics. Through his interactions in a crowded laboratory with fellow scientists—some decidedly anti-Christian—Alexander was brought up to date on how people thought about science and faith. His publisher had asked him to replace his book *Beyond Science*, and its completion kept getting pushed back. An entirely new book, *Rebuilding the Matrix*, was published in 2001, approximately fifteen years late.

The new book had the same aim as *Beyond Science*, but its material was completely different. Alexander meditated at length on the reasons why faith and science, once so closely related, had become understood as conflicting realms. He included chapters on the misuse of science in eugenics and on Galileo's conflict with scientific and church authorities. A lengthy section considered how Darwin's theory of evolution had become a source of conflict between science and faith. Alexander sought not just to defend Christianity but to rebuild the matrix of science within a theistic framework. He portrayed the two realms as complementary.

During the years he was writing this much-delayed book, Alexander got drawn into Christians in Science, an evangelical association of scientists. He was recruited to serve on the national board and then to edit a journal, *Science and Christian Belief.* "I'd always felt that my gifts were in apologetics, conveying the Christian message in an academically coherent manner."

Even so, he was looking to do more. His institute had a rule of retirement at age sixty. As that day drew near, he wondered what would come next. He had helped establish a series of lectures at Cambridge on faith and science, assisted by a three-year grant from the Templeton Foundation. Should they seek a renewal? "I had a dream of getting paid to write books." As much as he enjoyed laboratory science, his fundamental ambition had always been to tell the big story, to speak of his faith in a persuasive way. Encouraged by Templeton, he and close Christian colleague Bob White, a professor of geophysics at Cambridge, applied for a grant of several million dollars. They received it all. The Faraday Institute was launched with Alexander as director.

Just as he had hoped, directing Faraday left Alexander with more time to write. He had not thought of tackling the creation-evolution controversy since he was personally untroubled by its questions. As director of Faraday, however, he went out to give talks in churches on a regular basis. He found that the first questions people raised often had to do with Genesis and evolution. "I realized it was quite a question."

Looking for a book he could recommend, he wasn't happy. Some books were good on the science questions, and some were good on the biblical and theological questions, but he wanted a book that would do both. He concluded he would have to write it.

Creation or Evolution: Do We Have to Choose? came out in 2008. It is a thorough exposition of the case for evolution as the means of God's creation. The book is confident and magisterial. Alexander's expertise as a molecular biologist comes through most clearly in his explanation of the evidence for evolution in genomic studies.

The book offers much more than science, however. The breadth of Alexander's education enables him to begin with a robust doctrine of biblical creation and to offer a carefully reasoned suggestion for how a historical reading of Genesis could fit with what evolutionary science has revealed about human history. He also sharply rebukes intelligent design as bad science and bad theology, and he explains the evidence for the age of the earth that, he believes, makes the young earth creationist interpretation of Genesis untenable.

Although Alexander wades into such areas of controversy expressing strong, clear-cut beliefs, he insists that the heart of his mission is not to do battle with creationists or atheists. In Britain, young earth creationism remains a small minority opinion among Christians. Among scientists, at least, they are a negligible influence. And while the so-called New

Atheists have sold millions of books, Alexander thinks their media-fueled success is a short-term cultural phenomenon, no real threat.

"On the whole they have done us a lot of good, generating a huge amount of interest in science and religion. I'm sure we get far more people in our courses than we would have done otherwise. And we get invited to give talks with Dawkins in the title, 'The Dawkins Delusion,' for example, and lots more people come. It's been quite useful.

"But we don't see our mission is to engage or confront New Atheism. My view is that the New Atheism will die over a period of time as American politics changes, as the world stage changes, as certain people retire, and as people get tired of it. It is very hard to generate sustained interest in atheism because it's the absence of theism. It's hard to get people committed to something like that.

"If they were really wise they would do it the Swedish way: Keep quiet. Take religion out of the public domain. Let it die through materialism. That's real secularism. We're not secular as long as we have Dawkins around because he brings a lot of theology to the public and in the media."

If Alexander's ambition is not to combat the New Atheists, what exactly does he hope to achieve? It's a much grander goal. "Our ambition is to change the culture of the discussion between science and religion in the academic world through good scholarship and good publications. We want to critique the presumption that the conflict thesis is the only story in town. The conflict model was around long before Dawkins. He's just stirred it up. We want to educate people about the religious roots of science and explain what religion is claiming and what it is not claiming. We want to encourage an academically solid discourse that doesn't have people shouting at each other."

Science and faith are close cousins, he insists. They ought to be able to sit around a table and learn from each other.

11 Simon Conway Morris

The Convergence of Life

One of the last century's most dramatic intellectual clashes began in 1972 when a geology student at the University of Bristol in England, Simon Conway Morris, first encountered fossils from the Burgess Shale.

The Burgess Shale was reasonably famous already in the small but colorful world of paleontology. In the early twentieth century, a paleontologist from the Smithsonian, Charles Walcott, had discovered a treasure trove of extraordinarily well-preserved fossils high in the Canadian Rockies. Not just teeth and skeletons, but skin and organs and tentacles were visible. Over several summers beginning in 1909, Walcott excavated in a narrow band of rock—"little taller than a man, and not so long as a city block!"—as Harvard paleontologist Stephen Jay Gould would put it exuberantly in his best-selling book *Wonderful Life*.[1] From that small outcropping of rock, a lost world emerged.

Walcott procured approximately sixty-five thousand samples, some of which could simply be picked up off the ground where shale plates lay in drifts.[2] Collected amid spectacular mountain scenery, transported by horse to the valley below, then by train to the Smithsonian, these fossil specimens came to rest in drawers deep in the bowels of the institution. Walcott wrote scientific papers on some of them, but many others were never carefully examined. Walcott's administrative responsibilities (he was secretary of the Smithsonian) apparently prevented him from giving them the time they were due.

Walcott did, however, send small sample collections to interested museums, including one at the University of Bristol. Thus it came to be that, decades later, one of Conway Morris's teachers pulled out this collection to use for a lesson in interpreting fossils. Though he did not find the fossils particularly compelling, Conway Morris was intrigued by the whole subject and sought out Walcott's papers in the school library. Something told him—a hunch, an intuition, he would later write—that these fossils were important. He learned that Professor Harry Whittington at Cambridge University was in charge of a renewed research project. Conway Morris wrote to Whittington and was invited for an interview.

If you want to work toward a PhD in England, you do not apply to an institution so much as to a particular professor. This professor, if he or she accepts you, becomes your personal mentor and you, his or her apprentice. There are no classes; you learn your subject by following the master. Whittington interviewed Conway Morris in his grand office occupying one end of Cambridge University's Sedgwick Museum, a Victorian edifice crammed with fossils in glass cases and cabinets. Two temperamental opposites met. Whittington, according to Gould, was a careful, quiet scholar, while Conway Morris was a loner and a nonconformist, habitually an oppositional character. This was an era of student rebellion, and Whittington had heard from Conway Morris's teachers that he "sits in the corner of the library reading, and wears a cloak."[3] Whittington must also have detected ability. With whatever misgivings, he offered Conway Morris a chance to work with him on the Burgess Shale.

There was only one catch. Another student, Derek Briggs, had also applied and had been assigned to study the bivalve arthropods—creatures of some interest. The subject left over was worms. Whittington believed he could find money to support Conway Morris in his research, but it would have to be worms. To Whittington's relief and surprise, Conway Morris was delighted with worms.

In the fall of 1972, Conway Morris began at Cambridge, where he soon developed appendicitis, which led to a serious internal infection. When he was not sick he worked with Burgess Shale material collected by Whittington and brought to Cambridge. He was learning mastery of technique. By the spring of 1973, he and Briggs were deemed ready for the field.

For the purposes of storytelling, it would be attractive to describe the two young scientists traveling west, out of settled England into the sweeping wilderness of the Canadian Rockies, ascending the snowy scree of Mount Wapta and proceeding with hammers in hand to search for fossils. In point of fact, they traveled to Washington, DC, where they were introduced to scores of cabinets in unair-conditioned storerooms of the Smithsonian. They were meant to find promising material from Walcott's thousands of samples, pack up selected examples, and send them to Cambridge for study. It was a chore somewhat like cleaning out your grandmother's attic.

To that point, Whittington and other scholars had attempted to make a dent in this vast collection by selecting species that were well represented and thoroughly studying them. One at a time, they would identify and describe the creatures of a lost habitat. The fossils of the

Burgess Shale were known to come from the Cambrian, a geologic era about five hundred million years ago when the first small sea animals began to appear. Nearly all these creatures—trilobites, most famously—had become extinct. Studying the Cambrian meant learning how animals came to be before fish, before dinosaurs, before mammals, when small things scuttled on the ocean floor. The evolutionary assumption was that these were ancestors of creatures now living and that a smooth developmental history of life could be established.

By 1973 there was some reason to doubt whether these assumptions were correct. Whittington's first studies had found creatures that did not seem related to anything. Conway Morris, bearing his hunch that the Burgess fossils would prove important, wanted to gain as broad an understanding as possible of what worms had to offer. Worms represented "a fairly unconstrained concept"—all kinds of creepies and crawlies. Instead of selecting one or two well-represented fossils for study, Conway Morris went trolling through the entire archive, opening cabinets and drawers to see everything Walcott had collected. What he found was astonishing. "Weird and wonderful came out very quickly. I saw lots of rare stuff. It just popped up." Some of the fossils had to stay at the Smithsonian, but he was generously allowed to take a great many of them to Cambridge.

There he spent days and weeks and months in dark, cramped rooms, looking through a microscope. The fossils were small—many an inch in length, or less—and for purposes of comparison needed to be photographed, often under ultraviolet light, with the fossils tilted to a certain angle. Photographs did not show crucial details visible to the eye, however, so the fossils also had to be carefully sketched, using a special microscope attachment so the fossil image could be projected onto a piece of paper and traced. Further work involved excavation, by which millimeters of shale and fossil were painstakingly removed from the samples using a dentist's drill, revealing more of the fossil underneath. Some fossils were three-dimensional—he could excavate under an abdomen and discover claws, chip away a leg and find how it attached to the body.

By some process—possibly underwater landslides—the Burgess fossils had preserved features in far richer detail than a paleontologist dreamed of. But making sense of it was a painstaking labor of reconstruction. The fossils featured broken parts detached from each other, bodies squashed and distorted. Visualizing the original creature was like solving a jigsaw puzzle by M. C. Escher.

Part of the problem was that many of the creatures were unlike anything ever seen before. Conway Morris named one such *Hallucigenia* to denote its dreamlike character. When he showed a preliminary drawing to a colleague, he burst out laughing. (Further specimens were discovered later, revealing that Conway Morris's original drawings had the creature upside down, walking on spines protruding from its back and waving its feet in the air.)

Whittington provoked similar laughter at a meeting of the Palaeontological Society of Oxford when he showed a drawing of another Burgess creature. The laughter was unsettling, to say the least. What had set out to be an orderly march through a new set of fossils, placing each creature in its appropriate category, seemed to be turning into an Alice in Wonderland theme party. "Many of the animals from the Burgess Shale," Conway Morris would write years later, "look, to our eyes, to be very peculiar, if not downright bizarre."[4]

In 1976 and 1977 Conway Morris published his first scientific papers—five daring studies of creatures that seemingly fit no category. Some descriptions were tentative, and some—notably *Hallucigenia*—would turn out to be mistaken. But clearly, he had evidence of something completely unexpected, a riot of newness, breaking out with new forms that seemed to have no ancestors and no heirs. Conway Morris's understated scientific prose in describing *Nectocaris pteryx*, one of the new creatures, captures something of the moment: "The failure to resolve definitely the affinities of this creature need not be a source of surprise. Current research is showing that a number of species from the Burgess Shale cannot reasonably be accommodated in any extant phylum."[5]

———

During this same period, Stephen Jay Gould was becoming extremely famous both as a scientist and as a science writer. His subjects ranged widely, and his books sold well. He was particularly well known for his explorations of the theory of evolution. He and Niles Eldredge developed the idea of *punctuated equilibrium*, which stressed that evolutionary change happens not through a slow, gradual process but in fits and starts.

He was very interested in the work of Whittington, Briggs, and Conway Morris. According to *Wonderful Life*, he spent nearly two decades over beer and coffee discussing the Burgess Shale with the three principals. It was, he thought, "some of the most elegant technical work ever accomplished in my profession." He wrote that if he were to award the first Nobel Prize in paleontology (there is no such award), he would give it to these three men.[6]

In 1989, Gould published *Wonderful Life*, a breathless account of the Burgess Shale discoveries, declaring them to be "the world's most important animal fossils"[7] and heaping praise on the three scientists who reinterpreted them. A delight to read, the book made the Burgess Shale famous well beyond the academic groves of paleontology. The Cambrian explosion and its implications for evolutionary theory became part of popular vocabulary. Certainly, if scientific fame were his aim, Conway Morris could not have been more fulfilled. In 1990 he was elected to the Royal Society, the highest honor any British scientist can attain, apart from the Nobel Prize.

Wonderful Life is more than an account of scientific discovery. It provides a jumping-off point for Gould's thoughts on evolution. Ever since Darwin, evolution had been portrayed as plodding predictably upward, with a widening diversity of creatures spreading out in an evolutionary tree. In Gould's view, reality as revealed by the Cambrian explosion was quite different. New life-forms leaped into being in astonishing variety and profusion. They seemed to come out of nowhere, and most of them seemed to have vanished to the same place. Only a few passed down their attributes to other, later creatures. Most of them died out, not (apparently) because they were less fit to survive but simply (perhaps) through random circumstances. With the help of the Burgess Shale, Gould pictured evolution as utterly random. Famously, he said that if "life's tape" were replayed, the same result would never occur.[8] Human life in particular was a product of mere luck—"contingency," in Gould's terminology—and would not be expected to happen again under the same circumstances.[9]

"If you wish to ask the question of the ages—why do humans exist?" Gould concludes,

> —a major part of the answer, touching those aspects of the issue that science can treat at all, must be: because *Pikaia* survived the Burgess decimation. This response does not cite a single law of nature; it embodies no statement about predictable evolutionary pathways, no calculation of probabilities based on general rules of anatomy or ecology. . . . We are the offspring of history, and must establish our own paths in this most diverse and interesting of conceivable universes— one indifferent to our suffering, and therefore offering us maximal freedom to thrive, or to fail, in our own chosen way.[10]

The Conway Morris who began his PhD work at Cambridge in 1972 might have embraced Gould's interpretation. Gould's understanding was very close to Conway Morris's when he first began to interpret the Burgess Shale. But he was now married with two sons. And he had been reading and thinking.

Conway Morris's upbringing was "desperately uninteresting, even to me," he says. He grew up in Wimbledon, a suburb of London, and went to good private schools there. His father, a very successful solicitor who (unusually) ran his own practice, and his mother, an artist and a teacher, lived separately, though they never divorced. They were not particularly religious, but they attended church on special occasions. Nor were they scientific. Conway Morris seems to be the only family member who has pursued a career in science, and he can't recall being acquainted with any scientists growing up.

He did, however, develop a scientific hobby. When he was seven or eight years old, he was given a large book on prehistoric life, with colorful stamps of creatures that you could tear out and paste into the appropriate spot. Coincidentally, a friend had become very interested in collecting fossils. Conway Morris's mother patiently took the boys camping on the beautiful Dorset coast. (Their father proclaimed that he had lived in a tent in Egypt during WWII and would never enter one again.) There they happily hunted for fossils, finding many. Conway Morris "decided to become a paleontologist at the age most children are still determined to succeed as train drivers."[11]

He recalls, "The Natural History Museum in Kensington was just a tube ride away, and we used to take our fossils up to be identified. It is a vanished world, schoolboys getting attention in a major national museum." A few times, the museum regarded their finds as significant and asked to keep them. Conway Morris's university studies in geology and an academic career in paleontology developed naturally.

His father died suddenly when Conway Morris was just launching his Burgess research. Apparently, he learned, his father had developed a serious interest in Christian faith not long before he died, carrying on long conversations with a minister. But father and son never spoke of it.

Conway Morris says he cannot remember what sparked his interest in C. S. Lewis. "In the average week I pick up five or six books, and I might be lucky to read two. I may have picked up Lewis by chance."

Through Lewis, he was led into reading all Lewis's friends and influences: Dorothy Sayers, J. R. R. Tolkien, Charles Williams, and Owen Barfield, who were Lewis's contemporaries, and supremely G. K.

Chesterton, who lived and wrote prolifically a generation before Lewis. (Chesterton seems to have been the strongest influence if you can judge by prose style. Conway Morris's writing is robust and argumentative, maddeningly obtuse to his critics and flamboyantly exciting to his admirers, just like Chesterton's.)

These writers led Conway Morris to Christ. "Faith began to establish itself when I was doing my PhD, in a roundabout way, and it continued in a somewhat erratic fashion since then. It was a matter of personal assent. I can't see any other system which could possibly work. That may sound rather dry and desiccated, but I don't think so. They opened completely new worlds. They allow[ed] us to step outside ourselves, ask what it means to be human, why are we not animals anymore while clearly of animal derivation."

Nine years after Gould's *Wonderful Life*, Conway Morris published *The Crucible of Creation: The Burgess Shale and the Rise of Animals*, which differs substantially from *Wonderful Life*. Some of those differences have to do with fact. New discoveries and fuller consideration muted the radical exuberance of the Cambrian explosion. Some creatures from the Burgess Shale turned out to relate more closely to others than had been thought. The development of genomic studies was revealing that present-day creatures that seem utterly different are genetically cousins. It remained true that an explosion of life occurred—if you can call an explosion anything that takes millions of years. But the idea that new creatures appeared almost ex nihilo and became extinct willy-nilly, with little or no relation to other creatures, was not really accurate, Conway Morris wrote. ("A lot of the things that I thought turned out to be absolute nonsense," he told an interviewer in 2011.) "The idea that the Cambrian was awash with failed body-plans can now be abandoned."[12]

These were technical matters of concern primarily to paleontologists. On larger, interpretational issues, Conway Morris drew conclusions directly opposite to Gould's. Yes, life was contingent—nobody could doubt that. "Any historical process, be it the history of life over millions of years, or the story of a nation's development over several hundred years, must be riddled with contingent events. Their effect is, [Gould] maintains, to render almost any prediction of the future course of history a futile and redundant exercise."[13]

Conway Morris thought that was true only in the narrowest sense:

> While . . . the evolution of the whales is from the perspective of the Cambrian explosion no more likely than hundreds of other end points, the evolution of some sort of fast, ocean-going animal that sieves sea water for food is probably very likely and perhaps almost inevitable. Although there may be a billion potential pathways for evolution to follow from the Cambrian explosion, in fact the real range of possibilities and hence the expected end results appear to be much more restricted. If this is a correct diagnosis, then evolution cannot be regarded as a series of untrammelled and unlimited experiments. On the contrary, I believe it is necessary to argue that within certain limits the outcome of evolutionary processes might be rather predictable. . . . Put simply, convergence shows that in a real world not all things are possible.[14]

The term *convergence* refers to the observation that different evolutionary pathways often lead to near identical results. For example, saber-toothed tigers developed as mammals in North America, related to present-day lions, while very similar creatures developed in South America as marsupials, related to present-day kangaroos. There was a niche for fast, agile creatures with massive canines. Through two completely different ancestries, they developed nearly the same solution. "It is as if there is a sabre-tooth 'space,' waiting to be occupied."[15]

Another famous example is the human eye, which shares its complicated structure with other not closely related creatures, such as the octopus. Apparently they evolved independently but came to the same result.

Conway Morris's point, which he greatly amplified in the 2003 book *Life's Solution: Inevitable Humans in a Lonely Universe*, is that evolution has a direction. It may be random in the details but not in the outcome. In particular, he writes, evolution reveals that life develops intelligence and self-consciousness. Rerunning the tape, our world would develop creatures something like us again and again. Humans are inevitable.

This was a stunning and highly controversial argument. Gould, clearly stung, responded in *Natural History* magazine, disagreeing with Conway Morris's interpretation of the fossil record and, more pointedly, complaining that Conway Morris was ungrateful. He was

imperiously dismissive of my ideas. . . . I developed my views on contingency and the expanded range of Burgess diversity directly from Conway Morris's work and explicit claims, and I both acknowledged my debt and praised him unstintingly in my book. I even suggested— although it's surely none of my business—that Whittington, Conway Morris, and Briggs should receive the Nobel Prize for their exemplary work. Conway Morris is certainly free to change his mind, as he has done. Indeed, such flexibility can only be viewed as admirable in science. But it is a bit unseemly never to state that you once held radically different opinions and to brand as benighted, in some obvious and permanent sense, a colleague who holds the views you once espoused.[16]

The two would later meet amicably at scientific meetings, but they never talked directly about their differences, according to Conway Morris. Their interpretations could probably never be reconciled. Conway Morris's challenge spoke directly to a key metaphysical claim often made about evolution: that it is pointless and meaningless, utterly random, and therefore strips life of transcendent meaning. This view has certainly not gone away, but neither has the youthful paleontologist's challenge to it. Looking over a stack of applications for graduate school, Conway Morris remarks, "Convergence is becoming, heaven help me, almost popular."

———————

In Simon Conway Morris's distinguished career, he has pursued Cambrian fossils not just in Canada but also in China and Greenland. He has gazed at particular fossils for hours through a microscope, trying to make sense of them. Nowadays he focuses on making sense of a much wider vista: the whole history of life.

He has reached his early sixties, though with his dark and shaggy hair he doesn't look it. He works in the same building where Whittington first interviewed him: the Cambridge Department of Earth Sciences. A grand staircase ascends to the Sedgwick Museum; a narrow doorway beside it leads to less elegant offices and a coffee room, where oak and glass cabinets display hundreds of samples of British limestone, identified by quarry and region. Conway Morris's office is off a long corridor in this more utilitarian environment; it is, like many academics' offices, a warren with books and papers stacked on every surface, as though a fountain spewing paper had recently been turned off. Here Conway Morris reads—in every conceivable area of biology, it seems—and writes, using a fountain pen on unlined sheets of white paper.

He has not stopped being controversial. He provokes vociferous argument and sometimes even aggressive condemnations of his religious views in what purport to be scientific papers.[17] In *Life's Solution* he tried to account for this:

> Interpretations surrounding the brute fact of evolution remain contentious, controversial, fractious, and acrimonious. Why should this be so? The heart of the problem, I believe, is to explain how it might be that we, a product of evolution, possess an overwhelming sense of purpose and moral identity yet arose by processes that were seemingly without meaning. If, however, we can begin to demonstrate that organic evolution contains deeper structures and potentialities, if not inevitabilities, then perhaps we can begin to move away from the dreary materialism

of much current thinking with its agenda of a world now open to limit-less manipulation.[18]

Those last words hark back to Gould's interpretation of life as utterly random and his belief that we are utterly free to live in any way we see best. Conway Morris argues, instead, that evolution moves in a direction and that this direction reveals a deep structure built in to the cosmos. His understanding of biology is akin to physicists' anthropic principle, which notes that the physical universe is astonishingly well tuned to produce life. Conway Morris suggests that it is equally well tuned to produce complex life-forms and ultimately complex life-forms with intelligence and consciousness. (He does not say, though the implication is not hard to reach, that the universe is structured to bring forth creatures who can worship the Creator.) He is working to explain this view, so at odds with the meaningless materialism of many of his scientific peers, by delving deeper into biology. He aims to show it as a scientist, not a philosopher or a theologian.

Naturally, such a view provokes alarm. "Colleagues think I'm try-ing to smuggle in a creationist agenda, which I'm not, not least because if what I write turns out to be gloriously wrong, it's wrong. You can't get everything right, as I learned from my previous work. Emphatically, one doesn't want to use this as ammunition to be a Christian. These are not facts like electric fish. All they do allow you to show is that evolution navigates to particular solutions. One is allowed to ask, 'Why is the world constructed in this way to allow this to happen?' the same way that one might ask, 'Why is the world constructed so as to allow a periodic table?'"

Nor is he trying to say that the world exists just for the sake of pro-ducing human beings. "It's not emphatically trying to say, 'It's only about us.' It's about the whole biosphere, though only we, so far as we know, know that there is a biosphere. My dog doesn't show any interest in the biosphere."

Conway Morris is quite familiar with creationist and intelligent design literature, and he has no time for their claims. "If you happen to be a 'creation scientist' (or something of that kind) and have read this far," Conway Morris wrote in *Life's Solution*, "may I politely suggest that you put this book back on the shelf. It will do you no good. Evolution is true, it happens, it is the way the world is, and we too are one of its products. . . . Contrary to popular belief, the science of evolution does not belittle us."[19]

In his understanding of evolution, God's creation is incredibly rich and fertile, producing not just life but human life. He doesn't claim any proof of the existence of God, but he does think belief in God is congruent with what evolution reveals. More, he revels in the astounding complexity and beauty of the creation. In *Life's Solution* Conway Morris describes one life-form after another in intricate detail. He does so to make his point that life has direction, that "the evolutionary routes are many, but the destinations are limited."[20] He is one of a kind among scientists, quoting writers like Tolkien and Chesterton in his scientific tomes.

Conway Morris has attracted attention through another claim: he believes it very likely that we humans are alone in the universe. One cannot be sure, he writes, but given the special conditions that formed our earth, allowing life to begin and develop, it seems very likely that no life has developed on other planets. If it did develop, he thinks it almost certainly has produced intelligent life very much like us.

Conway Morris cannot write about the history of life without verging on areas that are frankly metaphysical. He draws the line, in his scientific writings, at theology. In other forums, where he is invited to speak of his faith, he goes over that line. In the prestigious 2007 Gifford lectures and in the 2005 Boyle lectures, he spoke directly to matters of faith. He sees a battle against those seeking to use science in opposing faith. He is unafraid to fight it.

For example, in speaking of the popular thesis that ours is only one of many "multiverses":

So peculiar and so finely balanced do the key physical constants appear to be that it is hardly surprising that many physicists have embraced the concept of not just one universe but a gadzillion of them tucked away behind black holes or hidden in other dimensions, ever present but ever invisible. And out of that gadzillion, well we are the lucky ones where everything turned out to be just, precisely right.

Theologians are suspicious, and so they should be. Alternative universes, forever invisible? This sounds like an area for debate by such as Albertus Magnus, Thomas Aquinas and perhaps especially William of Ockham [medieval theologians]. More topically, is this concept of multiverses so very far removed in our society from the inalienable belief in our society of unlimited "choice"?[21]

Near the end of the Boyle lecture, Conway Morris concluded that science, for all its value, comes in behind other ways of knowing truth: "Science when it treats creation as a true Creation, and thereby faces up to its responsibilities, may well be important. I expect [Robert] Boyle [founder of the lecture series] would have agreed. It seems ultimately, however, that it is the knowledge and experience of the Incarnation, the wisdom and warnings given by Jesus in the Gospels, and not least the Resurrection that in the final analysis are all that matters."[22]

12 John Polkinghorne
Putting Science in Its Place

Alone among the scientists profiled in this book, John Polkinghorne has no direct involvement in the creation-evolution debate. He has thoughts, of course—who doesn't?—but he is professionally a physicist who spent his scientific career searching for the elusive quark. That gave him no special insight into evolution and creation.

He is included because he offers a unique perspective on how science and faith work together. Having left an outstanding scientific career to become an Anglican priest, Polkinghorne combines an understanding of science and orthodox Christian theology more than any other single person.

———

Polkinghorne is every inch an Englishman: modest, plainspoken, polite, and understated. You would not notice him on the street. His wife having died a few years ago, he lives alone in a small, extremely ordinary house on the outskirts of Cambridge, without any visible sign that a few years ago he won the £1 million Templeton Prize. Now in his eighties, he has a very active mind, which he expresses with great clarity.

His thoughts have ranged so widely and so adventurously over the decades, it is hard to summarize them. Wherever his thoughts go, however, he expresses them tidily in short, cogent books, of which he has written five on physics and twenty-six on the relationship of faith and science. Most people do not find them a delight to read. Even when he is writing about faith, Polkinghorne expresses himself as though he were writing for a science textbook, in unadorned prose with no wasted words. To get something from his writing, you must concentrate on individual paragraphs or even individual sentences.

Likewise in conversation he speaks in balanced phrases. In a room of flamboyant personalities he might disappear, except that sooner or later someone would discover his superior competence. Polkinghorne's spare prose often drives to the heart of the issue.

He grew up in exquisitely ordinary circumstances in the English village of Street. His father, one of eleven children, left school at the age of fourteen to work for the post office. On his mother's side, his grandfather was a groom, training horses for a rich landowner. "We were lower-middle-class people with a concern for respectability," Polkinghorne wrote in his autobiography.[1] He never met a scientist or a mathematician when he was growing up; such people lived in another world.

His parents were deeply Christian people, though they rarely said much about it. Polkinghorne did not chafe at regular church attendance; their vicar was a good preacher who made Scripture come alive. "I cannot recall a time when I was not in some real way a member of the worshiping and believing community of the Church," Polkinghorne wrote.[2]

His mother loved to read—Dickens, particularly—and so did Polkinghorne, but he was exceptionally good at math. Before long his ability was noticed, and he was encouraged to attend schools where he could get more advanced instruction. Most first-class education in Britain came at private "public schools," but these were out of the reach of a humble postmaster. When he was ready for secondary school, however, Polkinghorne was accepted at the Perse School in Cambridge, a hybrid between a government school and a private one, subsidized so that his parents could afford it. He had to ride the train to get there and then take a long walk from the station.

Polkinghorne lost both of his siblings. Not long before he was born, his sister died at the age of six months because of an intestinal blockage. When Polkinghorne was twelve, his older brother, a Royal Air Force pilot, was lost during WWII. Perhaps as an only child Polkinghorne had an enlarged sense of being special. At any rate, he was fiercely determined to do well in school, obsessing over being at the top of his class.

Challenged by excellent teaching and smart fellow students at Perse, he soared. The result was a scholarship to study mathematics at Trinity College in Cambridge, perhaps the highest achievement open to any undergraduate mathematician in Britain. Isaac Newton, Niels Bohr, Ludwig Wittgenstein, and Bertrand Russell attended Trinity, which is especially well known for excellence in mathematics. "Scratch me and I'm Trinity," Polkinghorne says.

His first Sunday in college was a pivotal day. He attended Holy Trinity Church for an evening service sponsored by the Cambridge Inter-Collegiate Christian Union (ICCU). The preacher spoke on Zacchaeus, pointing out that Jesus passed through Zacchaeus's village only once on his way to Jerusalem. Had Zacchaeus failed to respond to Jesus then, he might not have had another chance. The preacher said the same might be true of them: they could not be sure whether they would have another opportunity to respond to Jesus. He invited them to come forward that night and commit their lives.

"I knew I had to go forward," Polkinghorne remembers. "At the time I would have counted that evening as being the moment of my definite Christian conversion."[3] It "led to a deeper personal commitment to Jesus

Christ as Lord; encouragement to serious and sustained study of scripture; the establishment of a regular pattern of times of prayer. These gifts have stayed with me throughout my life." As time went on he came to believe that he had been a Christian before then—that his going forward at church was a moment of deeper commitment rather than a conversion. And he would also come to regret the narrowness of the Cambridge CICCU, which frowned on drama and art and seemed fearful of encountering other points of view. "There was a certain bleakness that seemed to be expected of the faithful, which cast something of a shadow."[4]

Nevertheless, he spent his undergraduate years at Cambridge immersed in the CICCU fellowship. He met and fell in love with a fellow CICCU member, Ruth Martin, also studying mathematics. He went on for a PhD in physics and married Ruth shortly after he finished. Together the newly married couple traveled to Pasadena, California, where Polkinghorne had a postdoctoral fellowship at Caltech. From there he went to teach in Edinburgh for two years before finally returning to Cambridge. In Cambridge he would stay, except for short sojourns in Princeton, Berkeley, and Stanford in the United States and CERN in Switzerland.

———————

It is difficult to describe Polkinghorne's career in particle physics because the work involves highly technical mathematics that utterly mystifies ordinary people. He was extremely good at it, living during one of physics' golden periods, working out some of the fundamentals of the structure of matter. He was closely involved in the discovery of the quark.

Polkinghorne's first-name-basis colleagues included some of the most famous scientists of the twentieth century: Abdus Salam, Paul Dirac, Murray Gell-Mann, Richard Feynman, Stephen Hawking, and Steven Weinberg. Of that list, all but Hawking have received the Nobel Prize. Though Polkinghorne never achieved their level of fame, he was named a fellow in the Royal Society, Britain's highest scientific honor.

Nevertheless, in his late forties, Polkinghorne unexpectedly announced that he was leaving physics to become an Anglican priest. The move startled his colleagues, who wondered what was wrong. Polkinghorne insists that he was not dissatisfied with physics, not at all. He had suffered no unusual disappointments; he certainly had the option to continue in his coveted job as a Cambridge professor until retirement.

For years, though, he had thought he would move on before he turned fifty, perhaps into university administration. Polkinghorne says he believed he had done his best work in physics. "It's not true that you do your best work before you are twenty-five, but by the time you are forty-five you've probably done most of what you are going to do." He had watched other colleagues carry on, relegated to the second tier. "I didn't want people saying, 'Poor old John, he's not what he used to be.'"

As he pondered his options, talking to his wife, Ruth, and to close friends, the thought of ordination came to the fore. For one thing, his church had recently made him a lay preacher, which meant being sent out to lead services in country churches. He liked preaching. It was very different from lecturing. His only regret was that in the Anglican Church he could not preside over the Eucharist. More and more he found the Lord's Supper important to his faith, and so did Ruth. He wanted to lead a congregation in that, but it would require ordination.

During the same time period, a neighborhood Bible study was started by a former missionary and priest who was studying to be a psychotherapist. Ruth joined first, and after a year she urged John to come with her. He was reluctant to add another meeting to his week but soon found the studies extremely helpful. He gained a much greater appreciation of Scripture and its ability to expand one's mind. He wanted to go deeper.

The Polkinghornes's three children had left home or were about to. Ruth, who had devoted herself to raising them, decided to go back to school to train in nursing. It was a season for trying new things. Why not—radical thought—become a parish priest?

When Polkinghorne announced his decision to his fellow faculty, however, they reacted with some alarm and a great deal of curiosity. They knew of his faith, of course, but they couldn't imagine such a step.

For about eighteen months, "it was known that I was leaving science, but I hadn't yet left it." During that period he had many interesting conversations with colleagues, not only at Cambridge but also from around the world. They weren't so much interested in his ordination as they were in understanding why he was taking his faith to such an extreme.

"It's one thing to go to church on Sundays, but to give up a professorship and train for something else—that was a bit more than a gesture. It's a slightly odd thing to do. I think a lot of people realized I was a religious person but they didn't expect me to take it quite that seriously."[5] Most of the conversations were brief, over a cup of coffee, where "you can never say what you want to say." But over time he began to formulate the message he wanted to communicate.

Until then, it had not occurred to him that it needed saying. All his life he had appreciated both science and faith as complementary realms for seeking the truth. Combining the two had never been a struggle for him. He had assumed that it was a matter of sense, and now he realized "there is a bit of work to do. There is something to say. In particular, so many of my colleagues in the scientific world see religious faith as submission to irrational authority. You're just told what to do. Believe this. I wanted to show that I had motivations for my religious beliefs, like, for example, the resurrection, just as I had motivations for my scientific beliefs. Different kinds of motivation, different kinds of belief. The leap of faith is not a leap into the dark; it's a leap into the light.

"Part of attempting to engage with people is to lift their sights a bit. Say, look, the world is richer than a purely scientific view. We should take science very seriously, but that's a lunar landscape. It has no persons in it. You're a person. You know that music is more than vibrations in the air."

Polkinghorne had no idea that he would spend the rest of his life in such discussions. He planned to be a regular church minister, leading worship and preaching and visiting people in the hospital. In those coffee conversations, however, another vocation began to surface. It would be several years before it came to the fore.

––––––––––

As he trained to be a priest, Polkinghorne found that his hardest adjustment came with the realization that he was now nothing special. In the scientific community he had received instant respect. In the church his credentials barely got a nod. It did not seem to occur to anyone that his intellect should be treasured; on the contrary, his scientific background seemed to inspire less interest than if he had been a famous athlete. "The church didn't get the strategic nature of these issues." Rather, "it was just fine for those who were interested."

Polkinghorne did his seminary training in Cambridge. He was older than any of the other students and lived in the interesting bireality of turning from student to honored professor by walking down the street from one college to another. For two years he concentrated on learning Greek and Hebrew, studying the Bible and theology as well as learning the practical side of being a pastor. "It was odd becoming a student again after so many years as a university teacher. I was very used to standing up and talking for an hour, but it was much more difficult to listen to someone else for that length of time."[6]

There followed periods of apprenticeship in nearby Ely and then in Bristol at a working-class church. After a total of three years, plus two in theological college, Polkinghorne was deemed qualified to lead a parish. He seems to have expected interest from an urban or university church, where his intellectual gifts would be appreciated. Nothing of that kind came up. Instead, he was invited to become vicar—pastor—of a church in Blean, a small out-of-the-way town near Canterbury.

As Blean's vicar, Polkinghorne visited the home of anybody in the village who needed help or encouragement, whether he or she attended church or not. He led a regular service for healing prayer, a new and thought-provoking experience. He preached his way through the Bible, sticking closely to the text. As someone who had spent his entire adult life in the university, he adjusted to the very different rhythms and interests of rural England. He joined the Gardening Club. He even had time to write his first book on the relationship of science and faith, *One World: The Interaction of Science and Theology.* Polkinghorne has happy memories of Blean.

He soon began to recognize, however, that he needed more outlets for his intellect. People in Blean were not aware of the relations between science and faith, nor did they want to be. He had no one to talk with about such issues, no one on whom to regularly test his ideas. Even while far away from the university, he felt a growing compulsion to speak across the rift that divided Christians from the world of science.

Trinity Hall, another college in Cambridge, inquired about his becoming dean of the chapel. He accepted immediately. After he had been at Trinity Hall for three years, another venerable Cambridge college, Queens', asked Polkinghorne to become its president. That made for another transition. While dean of the chapel was pastor to students and faculty, the president of Queens' did a strictly secular job of leadership and administration. It was not exactly what he had hoped for. Polkinghorne still longed for the church to offer him a job with significant responsibilities, but by this time it was evident that the church was not interested. He accepted the job at Queens'. He had come full circle—to a university post where, at least in job description, his calling to ministry was irrelevant.

Clearly, though, he had been changed while making the circle—changed by having to explain his calling to unbelieving colleagues, changed by the rigorous study of theology and the Bible in the original languages, and changed by his exposure to the world outside the university. He had come to see his true vocation clearly. He was to be a hybrid, a "two-eyed" creature living in the university, who could see into and speak between realms that were hardly visible to each other, let alone on speaking terms—the realms of science and faith.

Polkinghorne has written about science and faith almost continuously since 1987, only occasionally repeating himself. He is a rare bird: a genuine scientist who has the training and the intellect to think deeply and theologically about what he has done.

At the core of Polkinghorne's thinking is the idea that there is only one world. He resists any attempt to divide religion from science in any ultimate way. They are both attempts to get at the truth of the world. They do so in different ways, and they may discover different aspects of the truth, but in the final analysis they must come together.

"Science should be part of everyone's world view," Polkinghorne wrote. "Science should monopolize no one's world view."[7] That is because science is one-eyed—it cannot see everything, even science itself. When Polkinghorne describes his scientific career, he often mentions the search for beautiful equations and the thrill and wonder of discovery. Science has nothing to say about beauty or wonder. They are inextricably part of science, but we need something more than science to explain and explore them.

"It is a remarkable fact that our minds have proved capable not just of coping with everyday experience but also of penetrating the secrets of the subatomic world. . . . Yet where in that world described by science can we locate the mind itself? . . . There is an ugly big ditch yawning between scientific accounts of the firings of neural networks, however sophisticated such talk may be, and the simplest mental experience of perceiving a patch of pink."[8]

Our awareness of pink—our consciousness of ourselves and our environment—is the most obvious and fundamental fact of our existence, says Polkinghorne. So are our awareness of making choices, our knowledge of our beliefs, our experience of pain or pleasure, our perception of color or form or music, our loves and our delights. These are mental realities that every child knows intimately. Yet they exist on the very outskirts of science simply because they are inherently wrapped in the individual's experience. We may agree that cutting ourselves is painful, but we really have no way to share pain or to know whether the pain we feel is the same as the pain others feel. There is no object called pain, only *my* pain. Consciousness cannot be objectified.

Polkinghorne's point is that science does not have the tools to explore a vast domain of obvious and fundamental reality. It is as though we were explorers who traveled to the most remote parts of the world but lived next door to an off-limits park—familiar because we see into it every day from our bedroom windows, but nonetheless impenetrable and unmapped. That park is the conscious mind. The scientist makes sense of the physical universe by meditating, experimenting, calculating, testing—but he cannot by the same techniques make sense of what he is doing, feeling, and thinking.

Polkinghorne is not willing to throw consciousness in a bin labeled "impenetrable" and forget about it. He insists that any comprehensive account of the universe must put these obvious and essential aspects of daily life in a prominent place—especially because they are so closely tied to our capacity to know *anything*. "An account of reality without a proper account of mind would be pitifully inadequate."[9]

That is what concerns Polkinghorne—an account of reality. Science, more than any other field, has contributed to it. But the larger project takes us beyond science. "We have to be realistic enough, and humble enough, to recognize that much of what is needed for eventual understanding is beyond our present grasp."[10]

"It would have been impossible to understand superconductivity without the revolutionary discoveries of quantum theory, which so substantially modified the Newtonian account of what matter is like. Consciousness is surely a much more profound phenomenon than superconductivity and its understanding may be expected to call for correspondingly much more radical revision of contemporary thought."[11]

Polkinghorne is thoughtfully dismissive of attempts to account for consciousness through materialist explanations. He thinks using computer processing as an analogy is hopeless. (Where, in these accounts, is the programmer?) He doubts that evolution fully accounts for the mind since it is not clear that consciousness has any survival value, and at any rate it is very hard to account for the survival value of, say, music or quantum mechanics. "Our scientific, aesthetic, moral and spiritual powers greatly exceed what can convincingly be claimed to be needed in the struggle for survival, and to regard them as merely a fortunate but fortuitous by-product of that struggle is not to treat the mystery of their existence with adequate seriousness."[12]

At the same time, he believes that our bodies—our brains, our synapses, our neural networks—are intrinsically involved in thinking. Given what we know about the genetic basis of mental illness, the effect of mind-altering drugs, the bizarre effects of brain damage, we can hardly think of the mind as a substance sitting on top of the brain. The mind must be in the brain, even while the brain does not begin to explain the mind.

It takes two eyes to begin to comprehend this reality. According to Polkinghorne, the full substance of reality cannot be understood without Jesus' resurrection.

For Polkinghorne the complex interfolding between the physical world and the mental world, between scientific experiment and questions of meaning and value, get captured in the so-called anthropic principle. This is comfortable territory for Polkinghorne, given his life as a physicist, for the anthropic principle rests on physical observations about the cosmos. In particular, it's the observation that a great many characteristics of the physical universe have to be almost exactly what they are in order for life as we know it to be possible.

For example, the fine structure constant, which measures the strength of electromagnetism, can't be even a single percentage point larger or smaller. The cosmological constant, which has to do with the strength of gravity, must be within a tolerance of one part in 10 to the power of 120. And there are many other examples in which the way the physical universe is structured "just happens" to make life possible. Slight variances—very slight variances—and the universe would be sterile.

"I already believed the world was God's creation," Polkinghorne says. "I just didn't realize God had to be so careful."[13]

Scientists and philosophers have lots of competing ideas about the implications of fine-tuning. Some conclude that there must be a Designer of the universe. Others say that fine-tuning means nothing more than that we humans have noticed that we live in a universe that produced humans. If it were another kind of a universe, we would not be here to observe it.

Polkinghorne takes a very moderate middle ground: that the fine-tuning of the universe for life is "a fact of interest calling for an explanation." He uses a parable from philosopher John Leslie: if a bullet hits a single fly on a big blank wall, one seeks an explanation. Pure randomness of a single bullet cannot be ruled out, but two other explanations seem more likely: either a great number of bullets were fired, or a marksman took careful aim.

Polkinghorne wants to take the parable one step further: if the fly had a button on its back that opened up a treasure chest of unthinkable riches, we would be all the more anxious for an explanation. That is what evolution suggests: our finely tuned universe was a rifle shot producing not just microbes, but Jane Austen and Albert Einstein. "The evolution of conscious life seems the most significant thing that has happened in cosmic history and we are right to be intrigued by the fact that so special a universe is required for its possibility."[14]

One way of explaining our finely tuned universe is some physicists' speculation about multiverses, the idea that an infinite number of universes exist in parallel, though inaccessible to each other. We just happen to be in the one that produced life. This explanation corresponds to the millions of bullets for Leslie's fly.

Another explanation is a divine Creator, who made a universe pregnant with life. This explanation corresponds to the marksman taking careful aim.

Polkinghorne says these explanations cannot be decided scientifically. No matter how the "multiple universe" explanation gets dressed up as science, it remains a metaphysical speculation. We need to look for other sources of understanding in order to say which is the best explanation of the "fact of interest" that we human creatures are here and that the universe seems perfectly fashioned to make us possible.

The anthropic principle, Polkinghorne says, reveals something very important about evolution. Polkinghorne describes evolution as the "shuffling exploration of possibilities" but notes that those possibilities are highly constrained by the physical world. Evolutionists talk about random variation—"chance"—but they don't necessarily comment on the environment of physical necessity within which chance operates. A flipped coin may land head or tails at random, but only head or tails. The structure of the coin limits the possible results. What we find in evolution is an environment that enables random variations to lead to life, to beauty, to consciousness, to personality, to Darwin the great scientist.

"You cannot, if you want to fulfill the role of Creator, simply bring into being more or less any old world and just wait a few billion years for something interesting to happen. . . . The interplay of chance and necessity requires the necessity to have a very special form if anything worthy (by our standards) to be called 'life' is to emerge."[15]

Polkinghorne accepts evolution. As a scientist he finds no difficulty with a material explanation of God's creation of life. After all, God holds the planets in place through gravity. He makes light through a nuclear explosion. Why should he not, if he likes, create life through "the shuffling explorations of possibility, which we choose to call 'chance'"?[16]

(Polkinghorne has never found it difficult to read the first chapters of Genesis as stories that illuminate fundamental truths rather than history.)

If evolution is the way in which God created the diversity of life, then Polkinghorne looks to see what evolution says about God himself. Evolution suggests a God working less like an engineer than a gardener. God's creation is dynamic. It tends, over vast stretches of time, to extend itself into ever-greater articulation, variety, and beauty. Does this vision of God diminish his power and majesty? Not according to Polkinghorne.

On the other hand, Polkinghorne knows that scientists are apt to get carried away with the overarching significance of their discoveries—to overinflate their universality. He applies this to his own field, physics. Physicists after Newton were convinced that they understood precisely how matter moved and interacted. Newton's discoveries resulted in a worldview that likened the universe to a windup clock, while assuring us that human freedom is an illusion. You could say that the overinflation of Newton's discoveries led to some of the worst aspects of the Enlightenment.

More than two hundred years passed before physicists realized that Newton had not quite got it right—that the clock of the universe was a very odd timepiece that we can describe using only very advanced mathematical equations. Its gears operate by probability, not linear necessity. The rationalistic modernism of Western civilization began to unravel about the same time that Newton's physics did.

Polkinghorne gently suggests that the great discoveries of biology in the past fifty years—and he agrees they are very great—may be exaggerated in a similar way: "We've explained genetics, so we can explain everything. We are on top of the wave."

Evolution explains a lot, uncovering "an astonishing drive to fruitfulness" in the world God has made. But evolution struggles to explain phenomena like consciousness, beauty, ethics, literature, art, religion, and science. Survival does not seem enhanced by any of these. Evolutionists may attribute them to accidental impulses left over from some primitive survival tactic, but that hardly seems like an adequate explanation for Van Gogh. "Darwinian ideas provide partial insight into the developing history of a fruitful world but it is certainly not known that they tell the whole story."[17]

———————

"It probably is true," Polkinghorne writes, "that physicists are a lot more open to questions of faith than others." They see a beautifully ordered world that inspires religiosity. "Einstein said that when he made a big discovery he felt 'like a child in the presence of the elders.' There is that sort of feeling to it and I think we should take that seriously."[18]

Polkinghorne also thinks that scientists are more open to faith than nonscientists since they don't operate in a postmodern world where there is no truth, only opinion. "Scientists have this feeling that there's a truth to be found, and that's very important to the exploration of religious belief."[19] Polkinghorne notes, however, that faith discoveries are more demanding than scientific ones. You might have to change your life:

> The fundamental question . . . is the question of whether the universe makes total and absolute sense—not simply the wonderful rational sense that science has discovered the physical world to possess, but an ultimate sense that embraces the whole range of human insight and aspiration—or whether it is a tale "told by an idiot"? In the end, the more we comprehend the universe, does it become more pointless or become more truly a cosmos, totally meaningful to us so that we are truly at home in it and not lone protestors against its absurdity? My instinct as a scientist is to seek a comprehensive understanding and I believe that it is my religious faith that enables me to find it.[20]

13 Conclusion

When I first contacted the eleven scientists I have profiled here, some reacted very suspiciously. They wanted to know my angle
and worried about being used as a foil for somebody's agenda. I understood and sympathized. The field has been so contentious, there has
been so much point scoring and name-calling, that thoughtful people
get gun-shy.

I told all of them the same thing: I was going to get out of the way
and let them tell their own stories. I wasn't going to try to referee who was
right and who was wrong. My goal was for readers to get to know them
and to understand their points of view.

I told them that I approached the subject of origins with well-deserved
humility. I know I am no expert. I know what I don't know—and it's a
great deal. The issues involved in creation and evolution are complicated
and highly technical, and they involve many disciplines.

If you go on the Internet, you will find plenty of people—from all points of view—who have apparently achieved perfect understanding and heap withering scorn on anyone who disagrees with them. I don't possess that kind of knowledge, and I don't think they really do either. Furthermore, I don't find that kind of contentiousness helpful. Some people seem to like it, but I think it sheds more heat than light.

I have tried to live up to my promises, to let the scientists tell their own stories. I have tried to give context where it was needed but not to pronounce right or wrong on anybody's beliefs. I hope I've succeeded.

But I don't want to leave the impression I don't have any opinions. In this concluding chapter I'm going to tell you what I think. Not that my opinions are terribly important. But I suspect some people will want to know.

———————

I have never had more fun than I did researching this book. I loved interviewing such interesting, knowledgeable, and smart people. Many of them, I think you'll agree, have fascinating stories. Without exception they possess outstanding credentials. Some are downright famous in their chosen fields of science. I was humbled, but even more I was fascinated. I learned a great deal.

Plus, I liked them all. It was evident that they were thoughtful, biblical Christians. They acted like it, treating me with genuine courtesy and giving me precious time. You can ask my wife: I came home happy every time. I genuinely appreciated the people I met.

How can you dismiss any of them? Are any not scientifically competent? Do any of their lives suggest that they are not serious about their faith? Are there any whose understanding is contemptible? In my judgment, they are serious people with something to say. All are brothers and sisters in Christ to whom I owe respect, even love, as we seek to understand these difficult matters.

The discussions may not be easy. Everybody can't be right. Disagreements are fundamental, so much so that it will be difficult to know where to begin. (Public debates are not helpful; they push people into defensive stances, and usually there's not much listening, only point-scoring.)

Those who speak contemptuously of others, or who refuse to listen, inevitably say—sincerely, I am sure—that they cannot compromise because truth is at stake. Indeed it is, but more than one truth is involved. The truth of Scripture is fundamental—a tenet that all these scientists would agree on. But so is the truth, frequently witnessed to in that Scripture, that all true Christians are part of the body of Christ:

In Christ we who are many form one body, and each member belongs to all the others. (Rom. 12:5)

The eye cannot say to the hand, "I don't need you!" (1 Cor. 12:21)

Be completely humble and gentle; be patient, bearing with one another in love. Make every effort to keep the unity of the Spirit through the bond of peace. (Eph. 4:2–3)

Get rid of all bitterness, rage and anger, brawling and slander, along with every form of malice. Be kind and compassionate to one another, forgiving each other, just as in Christ God forgave you. (Eph. 4:31–32)

In humility consider others better than yourselves. (Phil. 2:3)

Clothe yourselves with compassion, kindness, humility, gentleness and patience. (Col. 3:12)

Do these verses not apply when the subject is evolution and creation? Yet these qualities of love have not consistently marked our discussions. We have seen a great deal of haughty behavior. We need more humble listening, patient discussion, and gentle disagreement. The good lives of all these scientists, along with the unconditional truth of the Bible, insist on it.

———————

As stated in the introduction, our eleven scientists, fall into one of three camps:

1. *Young earth creationists*, who believe that the world is less than ten thousand years old and that Noah's flood explains most of the geology and fossil distribution that we see today. They also insist that the species of life are not all cousins but were created separately.
2. *Intelligent design creationists*, most of whom believe that the earth is billions of years old but that evolution cannot explain the development of life. Some intelligence must have intervened.
3. *Evolutionary creationists*, who believe that God created life, using evolution. They believe that all creatures are cousin to each other and that the process of variation and selection produces gradual change over millions of years.

Try to evaluate these three contradicting schools of thought, and you will find a great deal of back-and-forth argument over details. Somebody says ice core samples from Siberian lakes reveal a year-by-year record that goes back hundreds of thousands of years. No, somebody else says, other studies show that it's no such thing. Another person proclaims that multiple parts of the cellular flagellum motor have stand-alone uses. No, someone else says, none of those parts has been shown to have independent functions.

It is almost impossible for a layperson to evaluate these claims. If you try, you will find yourself submerged in an endless cascade of claim and counterclaim, with no simple way to tell whose claims are valid. You'll get lost in the technical data.

You have to look at the bigger picture. When you do, you find that each of the three schools has its particular strengths and its particular problems. These are the strengths and weaknesses that ultimately determine which school you believe in.

Here's how I see each one:

Young earth creationism's strength is a fundamental commitment to the Bible. Young earth creationists make a strong, commonsense case for a literal, historical reading of the first chapters of Genesis. It's not just a matter of the seven days of creation as twenty-four-hour cycles. It's also the literal reading of the genealogies, adding up to something close to six thousand years since Adam. And very crucially it's a literal reading of Noah's flood. These readings fit well with traditional Christian doctrines of the fall as traceable to Adam and Eve, and of the origins of sin and death in the fall. Young earth creationism (YEC) offers a consistent and familiar picture within the pages of the Bible.

YEC's greatest problem is that it doesn't match up with the world we live in, as scientists observe it. The biggest and most obvious issues are with geology. A universal flood occurring a mere five thousand years ago should leave massive evidence behind. After all, geologists see very clear evidence of local floods that took place twelve thousand years ago in eastern Washington, including boulders transported five hundred miles. But geologists say they don't see any evidence whatsoever of a global flood. Rather, they are quite sure that rock deposits and the fossils found in them were laid down over hundreds of millions of years.

YEC has proposed a bold narrative to make sense of flood geology, but it's only an outline. Few geologists take it seriously, and YEC doesn't have the money or the laboratories—or the scientists—to fill in the gaps. An additional problem is that YEC has so far barely addressed the avalanche of new biochemical and genomic information, which hugely strengthens the evolutionary case that all life is related.

Perhaps YEC *could* address these problems. But as it stands YEC presents a stark choice: you can uphold a traditional belief in the literal, historical reading of Genesis, but only at the cost of rejecting mainstream science. Yes, you can become a creation scientist, but there really isn't much science there: no labs, no experiments. The only career in science you can aspire to is teaching about creation science.

Intelligent design's strength is its assault on the New Atheists and their assertion that science proves that there is no God. When Phillip Johnson first read Richard Dawkins, he at once saw the fallacies in Dawkins's logic and had the rhetorical skill to call his bluff. ID draws support from people who have rejected YEC as too antiscience but question the good faith of atheistic evolutionists. ID also draws on people's intuitive sense that life is far too complex to have happened by accident. It speaks positively of science while undermining the materialist propaganda of some scientists.

ID's greatest problem is its wholesale rejection by mainstream science. ID tries to offer scientific proof that evolution is a failed theory, incapable of explaining complex life-forms. Although ID advocates like Michael Behe think they have succeeded in the proof, almost no other scientists agree. It is very difficult to prove a negative, which is what ID proposes to do.

Furthermore, though ID proponents claim that science can be done on the basis of ID principles, so far none has been done. ID seems to have become a philosophical position, detached from the Bible and from the practice of science.

Evolutionary creationism's strength is the flip side of YEC's. Within the world of scientific investigation, evolutionary creationism offers a coherent view. Scientists from every kind of faith and philosophy join in its scientific conclusions. Evolutionary creationism rejects atheistic evolution in favor of a view that evolution is God's way of creating. It stresses the traditional doctrine of God's immanence. Since God is intimately involved in the workings of the physical universe, his presence and power can be seen in the workings of evolution, evolutionary creationists say.

That enables them to offer a deep appreciation of science and a robust doctrine of creation.

Evolutionary creationism's greatest problem is the Bible. Evolution tells a story about our planet, and it is far from obvious that it fits the story we learn from Scripture. In evolution's story, creation requires billions of years, and the sequence of creatures does not match the traditional historical reading of Genesis 1. Evolution's story knows nothing of an Adam and Eve. It seems to suggest that humanity originated in a tribe of thousands of individuals, not just two. Furthermore, Adam's sin—the fall that spread sin and death throughout the world—has no counterpart in evolution's story. Evolution requires that pain and death have been part of creation from the beginning.

Evolutionary creationists have only begun to take this challenge with full seriousness. Biblical scholars offer a number of very serious proposals for rereading Genesis, and it may be that in time a new understanding will emerge that is actually stronger and deeper than the traditional, literal historical reading. For now, though, evolutionary creationists are comfortable in the world of science and can uphold a robust doctrine of creation within it. Their understanding of Genesis, however, is very much a work in progress.

I have briefly reviewed these strengths and weaknesses, as I see them, in order to emphasize that no one point of view is without merit, nor does any one point of view rise triumphant over all weaknesses. Christians seek the truth, both in science and in the Bible. That search is not simple. We need each other, to critique each other and challenge each other.

For myself, while respecting those who hold all three positions and seeing both strengths and weaknesses in all three positions, I am most hopeful for the evolutionary creationists. Let me explain why.

I start with the young earth creationists. Like any evangelical

Christian, I believe that the Bible is authoritative. And the YEC case for a literal, historical reading of Genesis is strong. That is not to say that theirs is the only way to read those Scriptures. Through the centuries, Christians have often read Genesis in other ways. But the literal, historical reading is certainly for me, with my upbringing, the most obvious way to take those passages. Every detail doesn't fit perfectly—there are difficulties and mysteries. But if I had nothing else to go on, I would accept a YEC interpretation of Genesis.

However, when your reading of a crucial Bible passage doesn't accord with reality, it is surely your duty to look again. This doesn't mean that science trumps Bible. It means that all biblical interpretation is fallible, and you need to make sure you are not jumping to conclusions.

For example, you could read Psalm 103:3 and conclude that since God heals all our diseases, a Christian (or a Jew) can never be sick. Some people have, indeed, drawn that conclusion. But noticing that the members of your church do get sick, you should review your interpretation.

That's how it is with young earth creationism. They say the earth is very, very young. But the earth doesn't look young. It looks very, very old. The more we examine it, the stronger this evidence for the age of the earth appears to be.

I am no expert, but I listen to scientists and don't find much ambiguity in their conclusions. Multiple lines of evidence, in physics, astronomy, geology, and paleontology, suggest a world that is billions of years old.

It's like this: I meet a very old man. He has deep lines all over his face, he walks with a stoop, and his hair is white. I ask him how old he is. "Oh," he says, "I was born forty-two seconds ago, just before you came into the room!"

It would be very hard for me to prove him wrong. In all honesty, however, I am going to find it very hard to take him seriously. That is how scientists feel when young earth creationists say that the world is six thousand years old. (Six thousand years, by the way, is about one-millionth of the age that scientists calculate for the earth—the equivalent of forty-two seconds for an eighty-year-old man.)

I do not take science lightly. The character qualities of the scientific community are good. Dishonesty or intellectual laziness is simply not tolerated. Members voluntarily check each other's work. There is a rigorous attempt to weed out error. These character qualities reveal something of science's beginnings in Christian faith.

Make no mistake, the Bible is my primary authority. But science has authority, too, and I am not eager to disregard it. I think we should be very wary of building our faith around a position that alienates us from the entire scientific community.

Is it possible that there is another way to read Genesis? Historically, great theologians did—Augustine, for example. And today, many Bible scholars of very conservative beliefs are reading Genesis in other ways, not because of science but because of recently discovered Middle Eastern literature from roughly the same period. These discoveries have caused scholars to wonder whether our literal historical reading would have made any sense at all to the original readers. They had different questions than we do, which Genesis was intended to answer.

I am not endorsing these newer readings—I just don't know enough—but I am ready to say that I don't think YEC has a monopoly on faithful, thoughtful ways to read Genesis. The earth appears to be very old. Just as with that eighty-year-old man, I think it probably is.

––––––––

What about intelligent design? It allows for an old earth and even (in the case of Michael Behe) the cousinly relationship of all living things. It seeks to be part of science.

ID has two components that I think are very helpful. One, as I have already noted, is its challenge to atheistic materialism posing as science. The other is its recognition of design.

I truly don't think design is controversial. All creatures are cleverly put together, a wonderful fit for their environment. Their components are ingenious. The best engineers in the world can only admire them and try to imitate them.

The controversial questions are these: Did anybody design the design? Or did the design come out of an unsupervised physical process that innovates by randomly casting up a million alternatives and letting them live or die depending on their fitness? Is the beauty we see in nature the result of an accident or a reflection of an intelligence involved in creation? Does the design fit into a larger purpose, or is it fundamentally meaningless?

Atheistic materialists like Richard Dawkins have ready answers to these questions: It's all meaningless. It just happened by accident. Nothing was planned. But that is not a scientific conclusion. It is a metaphysical assertion. Could anyone design an experiment to test any of the questions in the preceding paragraph? I don't think so.

It is at this point I begin to have trouble with ID, for ID claims to answer these questions purely on a scientific basis. And they claim to make a slam-dunk case. I won't go into the details of their case; I'll only say that it turns out not to be a slam-dunk case since it has convinced almost no scientists.

Personally, I doubt whether this is a realm for scientific proof at all. Science is good at telling us how something works. Who stands behind it is more a question for historical investigation and perhaps philosophy and theology.

ID proponents are a varied group. For example, Fazale Rana takes a very different approach from Michael Behe. It seems to me that some ID proponents have taken the wrong moves and put themselves in a dead end, doing what is fundamentally philosophical work while calling it science. At any rate, they have certainly lost whatever hope they once had of creating a science of intelligent design. The gulf between their position and that of the scientific community is as wide as can be. Wanting as I do to bring science and faith together, ID doesn't seem a promising approach.

It may be, as Michael Behe suggests, that in the long run biology will have to rethink. Perhaps John Polkinghorne is right to suspect that the present understanding of evolution is too simple and may be enriched (and complicated) by further discoveries. Simon Conway Morris points to an understanding of evolution that is far more easily understood in terms of design and purpose. In these ways, it's possible to imagine some of ID's ideas taken up again in a different form. In the present, though, it seems to have reached a dead end.

———

In ID I see confusion about mechanism and meaning. That confusion is not just in ID. It's certainly there in YEC arguments that evolution is necessarily a godless process because it relies on chance, and equally in atheistic materialist arguments that evolution is necessarily a godless process because it relies on chance. Indeed, the whole Western world has been infected by the Enlightenment paradigm suggesting that if you understand how something works mechanically, you have eliminated the supernatural. According to this view either God is at work, or physical processes are doing their work—it can't be both.

Any reflection on God's immanence—or on God's activity in the Bible—will explode this point of view. God is present and powerful everywhere. He is active and awesome in the thunderheads that sail through the skies, in the growth of seeds that work in the darkness underground, and in the actions of secular governments. The Bible says this again and again: God is personally active in all creation.

The example of the teakettle, which Ard Louis related, makes the point that we can describe phenomena at multiple levels. The water is boiling because of the heat transfer effects of exploding hydrocarbons working on a liquid that turns to a gas. The water is boiling because we want to make a cup of tea. Both explanations are equally true.

Even better is the example of a book. We can describe the book in terms of its physical components: the binding, the paper, the ink—all of which have complicated chemistry behind them. We can describe the book in terms of its manufacture: the process by which machines printed and bound it. We can describe the book in terms of the alphabet: a complex set of symbols. We can describe the book in terms of language, with its syntax and grammar and vocabulary. We can describe the book in terms of its style and form, whether fiction or nonfiction, essay or narrative. We can describe the book in terms of its meaning: what ideas in the mind of a writer it communicates to a reader—even when the writer has never had physical proximity to the particular book in question!

You can equally describe our world in different terms: its chemistry, its physics, its geography, its creatures, its ecology, and the purpose it serves for its Creator. Each of these levels is equally true, and no one of them exhausts the meaning of the world.

For certain scientists to say they have studied the origins of life and discovered that it is just a matter of chemistry is like certain printers saying that they have learned what inks were used to print *War and Peace* and now understand everything about it. The world of knowledge is a lot wider than that.

Scientists, as Fazale Rana noted, are very well trained but not very well educated. They know how to do science very well. They don't necessarily understand how it fits into the wider world. And like all of us, they tend to see no farther than the end of their noses. Most are interested in what science says and not much further.

———

If it is among evolutionary creationists that I see the greatest hope, much of the reason is that they seem ahead of the others in understanding the multilayered nature of reality. They are comfortable in science, and they have been learning to incorporate the doctrine of God's immanence into their understanding of the world.

Those I have talked with show a widening awareness of the need to live more deeply in Genesis. Rereading Scripture with new eyes is inevitably a challenging enterprise. No one should underestimate the difficulties. But some have done it before to great profit—think Martin Luther. If evolutionary creationists stimulate fresh, humble, faithful understandings of Genesis that enable us to tell God's creation story anew, marrying biblical revelation to scientific understanding, we will gain. That is a big *if,* but I am hopeful.

My sense of hope depends on the whole Christian community, not just one faction. If we continue to attack each other, and if there is no thoughtful dialogue between people of goodwill and excellent understanding, we will continue to lose.

But I am hopeful . . .

That young people will become scientists without fear of losing their faith but instead will feel excitement for unraveling God's secrets written in his creation.

That we will understand the Bible in new, rich ways as its intersection with God's revelation in creation is revealed.

That the church will not be divided over these issues, but that various points of view will embrace each other as they seek to understand the truth.

That the church will be faithful to Scripture—not married to a particular interpretation but deeply committed to study, understand, and follow God's Word.

That Christians will see science as a gift from God, letting humans participate in the extraordinary beauty and effectiveness of his creation.

That suspicion and defamation will diminish so much that people will be surprised and dismayed whenever they hear insulting comments made by one side about the other.

That science and faith will understand that they are allies, working toward a comprehensive understanding of everything. There is so much we have learned—libraries full—but so much more that is still to be learned!

Acknowledgments

I am deeply grateful for the support and encouragement offered by Kurt Berends and Michael Gulker through the Colossian Forum. Without their help, I doubt I could have written this book.

Dean Anderson, Harold Fickett, David Graham, and Philip Yancey read *The Adam Quest* in manuscript, making helpful suggestions.

Notes

Chapter 1   Introduction

1. Rudolf Bultmann, "New Testament and Mythology," in *Kerygma and Myth: A Theological Debate*, ed. H. W. Bartsch, trans. R. H. Fuller (New York: Harper & Row, 1961), 5, http://www.rochester.edu/College/REL/faculty/wierenga/REL111/outlines/miracles.html.

Chapter 2   Kurt Wise: A Warrior for Truth

1. Jonathan Rée, "Evolution by Jerks," *New Humanist* 118, no. 1 (Spring 2003), http://newhumanist.org.uk/598/evolution-by-jerks.
2. Stephen Jay Gould, "Nonoverlapping Magisteria," *Natural History* 106 (March 1997), 16–22, http://www.stephenjaygould.org/library/gould_noma.html.
3. Steven A. Austin, John R. Baumgardner, D. Russell Humphreys, Andrew A. Snelling, Larry Vardiman, and Kurt P. Wise, "Catastrophic Plate Tectonics: A Global Flood Model of Earth History," Washe (ed.), *Proceedings of the Third International Conference on Creationism*, 609–621, http://www.icr.org/article/catastrophic-plate-tectonics-flood-model/.

4. Kurt Wise, *Faith, Form, and Time* (Nashville: B&H Publishing Group, 2002), 201.
5. K. P. Wise, "Baraminology: A Young-Earth Creation Biosystematic Method," *Proceedings of the Second International Conference on Creationism*, R. E. Walsh and C. L. Brooks, eds., vol. 2 (Pittsburgh: Creation Science Fellowship, 1990), 345–58.

Chapter 3 Todd Wood: A Simple Truth Seeker

1. In 2013, after this chaper was written, Bryan College announced that CORE was closing.

Chapter 4 Georgia Purdom: A Passion to Teach

1. Edward Rothstein, "Adam and Eve in the Land of the Dinosaurs," *New York Times*, May 24, 2007.

Chapter 7 Mary Schweitzer: Digging Dinosaurs

1. Jack Horner and James Gorman, *How to Build a Dinosaur* (New York: Dutton, 2009), 69.
2. Ibid., 76.
3. Ibid., 79.
4. Ibid., 80–81.
5. The story of these nesting sites is told in *Walking on Eggs: The Astonishing Discovery of Thousands of Dinosaur Eggs in the Badlands of Patagonia* by Luis Chiappe and Lowell Dingus (New York: Scribner, 2001).

Chapter 8 Darrel Falk: Putting the Pieces Back Together

1. Darrel Falk, *Coming to Peace with Science* (Downers Grove, IL: IVP, 2004), 19.
2. Ibid., 19–20.
3. Ibid., 21.
4. Ibid., 22.
5. Ibid., 57.
6. Ibid., 231.
7. Ibid.
8. Ibid., 43.
9. Ibid., 24.
10. Ibid., 232.
11. Ibid., 222.

12. Ibid., 227.
13. Ibid., 25.
14. Ibid., 232.
15. Francis Collins, *The Language of God* (New York: Free Press, 2006), 20.
16. Peter Boyer, "The Covenant," *New Yorker*, September 6, 2010, http://www .newyorker.com/reporting/2010/09/06/100906fa_fact_boyer?currentPage=3.
17. Collins, *The Language of God*, 31.
18. Falk, *Coming to Peace with Science*, 233–34.

Chapter 9   Ard Louis: Evangelical Science

1. Ard Louis cited in *Test of Faith: Spiritual Journeys with Scientists*, ed. Ruth Bancewicz (Eugene, OR: Wipf & Stock, 2010), 71.
2. Ibid., 72.

Chapter 10 Denis Alexander: Speaking the Scientist's Language

1. Denis Alexander cited in *Real Scientists, Real Faith*, ed. R. J. Berry (Oxford, UK: Monarch Books, 2009), 29.
2. Ibid., 35.
3. Ibid., 36.
4. Ibid., 43.

Chapter 11 Simon Conway Morris: The Convergence of Life

1. Stephen Jay Gould, *Wonderful Life* (New York: W. W. Norton, 1989), 69.
2. "Charles Doolittle Walcott," Burgess Shale Geoscience Foundation, http:// burgess-shale.bc.ca/discover-burgess-shale/charles-doolittle-walcott.
3. Gould, *Wonderful Life*, 142.
4. Simon Conway Morris, *The Crucible of Creation* (Oxford, UK: Oxford University Press, 1998), 173.
5. Conway Morris cited in Gould's *Wonderful Life*, 146–47.
6. Gould, *Wonderful Life*, 16, 84.
7. Ibid., 23.
8. Ibid., 48.
9. Ibid., 299.
10. Ibid., 323.
11. Conway Morris cited in *Real Scientists, Real Faith*, ed. R. J. Berry (Oxford, UK: Monarch Books, 2009), 214.

12. Ibid., 218.
13. Conway Morris, *Crucible of Creation*, 99.
14. Ibid., 202.
15. Conway Morris cited in *Real Scientists*, 219.
16. Simon Conway Morris and Stephen Jay Gould, "Showdown on the Burgess Shale," *Natural History* magazine 107, no. 10 (1998–99): 48–55.
17. *Real Scientists*, 212.
18. Simon Conway Morris, *Life's Solution* (Cambridge, UK: Cambridge University Press, 2003), 2.
19. Ibid., xv.
20. Ibid., 145.
21. Simon Conway Morris, "The Boyle Lecture 2005: Darwin's Compass: How Evolution Discovers the Song of Creation," *Faith* (November–December 2005), http://www.faith.org.uk/publications/Magazines/Nov05/Nov%2005%20Darwins%20Compass%20How%20 Evolution%20Discovers%20The%20Song%20of%20Creation.pdf.
22. Ibid.

Chapter 12 John Polkinghorne:
Putting Science in Its Place

1. John Polkinghorne, *From Physicist to Priest* (London: SPCK, 2007), 4.
2. Ibid.
3. Dean Nelson and Karl Giberson, *Quantum Leap* (Oxford, UK: Monarch Books, 2011), 27.
4. Ibid., 28.
5. Polkinghorne cited in *Test of Faith: Spiritual Journeys with Scientists*, ed. Ruth Bancewicz (Eugene, OR: Wipf & Stock, 2010), 83.
6. Polkinghorne, *From Physicist to Priest*, 86.
7. John Polkinghorne, *Beyond Science* (Cambridge, UK: Cambridge University Press, 1996), 20.
8. Ibid., 53.
9. Ibid., 72.
10. Ibid., 73.
11. Ibid., 65.
12. Ibid., 64.
13. Nelson and Giberson, *Quantum Leap*, 113.
14. Polkinghorne, *Beyond Science*, 88.
15. Ibid., 81.
16. Ibid., 77.

17. Ibid., 79.

18. Polkinghorne cited in *Test of Faith*, 87.

19. Ibid., 88.

20. Polkinghorne, *Beyond Science*, 101.

Works Cited

Alexander, Denis. *Beyond Science*. Philadelphia: A. J. Holman, 1972.

———. *Creation or Evolution: Do We Have to Choose?* Oxford, UK: Monarch Books, 2008.

———. *Rebuilding the Matrix: Science and Faith in the 21st Century*. Grand Rapids: Zondervan, 2003.

Bancewicz, Ruth, ed. *Test of Faith: Spiritual Journeys with Scientists*. Eugene, OR: Wipf & Stock, 2010.

Behe, Michael. *Darwin's Black Box: The Biochemical Challenge to Evolution*. New York: Free Press, 1996.

———. *The Edge of Evolution: The Search for the Limits of Darwinism*. New York: Free Press, 2007.

Berry, R. J., ed. *Real Scientists, Real Faith*. Oxford, UK: Monarch Books, 2009.

Boyer, Peter J. "The Covenant." *New Yorker*, September 6, 2010.

Bultmann, Rudolf. "New Testament and Mythology." In *Kerygma and Myth: A Theological Debate*, ed. H. W. Bartsch, trans. R. H. Fuller. New York: Harper & Row, 1961, 5, http://www.rochester.edu/College/REL/faculty/wierenga/REL111/outlines/miracles.html.

Collins, Francis. *The Language of God*. New York: Free Press, 2006.

Conway Morris, Simon. "The Boyle Lecture 2005: Darwin's Compass: How Evolution Discovers the Song of Creation." *Faith* (November–December 2005), http://www.faith.org.uk/publications/Magazines/Nov05/Nov%20 05%20Darwins%20Compass%20How%20Evolution%20Discovers%20 The%20Song%20of%20Creation.pdf.

———. *The Crucible of Creation: The Burgess Shale and the Rise of Animals*. Oxford, UK: Oxford University Press, 1998.

———. *Life's Solution: Inevitable Humans in a Lonely Universe*. Cambridge, UK: Cambridge University Press, 2003.

Conway Morris, Simon, and Stephen Jay Gould. "Showdown on the Burgess Shale." *Natural History* 107, no. 10 (1998–99): 48–55.

Dawkins, Richard. *The Blind Watchmaker*. New York: W. W. Norton, 1986.

Denton, Michael. *Evolution: A Theory in Crisis*. Bethesda, MD: Adler & Adler, 1985.

Falk, Darrel. *Coming to Peace with Science: Bridging the Worlds Between Faith and Biology*. Downers Grove, IL: IVP, 2004.

Gould, Stephen J. *Wonderful Life: The Burgess Shale and the Nature of History*. New York: W. W. Norton, 1989.

Horner, Jack, and James Gorman. *How to Build a Dinosaur: Extinction Doesn't Have to Be Forever*. New York: Dutton, 2009.

Johnson, Phillip. *Darwin on Trial*. Downers Grove: IVP, 1993.

Nelson, Dean, and Karl Giberson. *Quantum Leap: How John Polkinghorne Found God in Science and Religion*. Oxford, UK: Monarch Books, 2011.

Polkinghorne, John. *Beyond Science: The Wider Human Context*. Cambridge, UK: Cambridge University Press, 1996.

———. *From Physicist to Priest: An Autobiography*. London: SPCK, 2007.

Rana, Fazale, and Hugh Ross. *Origins of Life: Biblical and Evolutionary Models Face Off*. Colorado Springs: NavPress, 2004.

Ross, Hugh P. *The Creator and the Cosmos*. Colorado Springs: NavPress, 1993.

Wise, Kurt P. *Faith, Form, and Time: What the Bible Teaches and Science Confirms About Creation and the Age of the Universe*. Nashville: B&H Publishing Group, 2002.

Wood, Todd Charles, and Megan J. Murray. *Understanding the Pattern of Life: Origins and Organization of the Species*. Nashville: Broadman and Holman, 2003.

Index

Turkey, Alexander and, 158, 160–162
Tyrannosaurus rex, 109

U–Z
Understanding the Pattern of Life (Wood and Murray), 40
United Kingdom, gap year for students, 156
universe, fine-tuned for life, 83
University of Bristol, 168
University of British Columbia, 121
University of Chicago, 14–15
University of Georgia, 90
University of Pennsylvania, 65–66
University of Virginia, 90
   Wood at, 34–36
university, worldview of, 143
Utrecht University, 142
Verwer, George, 156
vitamin C, gene regulation of, 98–99
Walcott, Charles, 167–168
Wall Street Journal, 75
watchmaker, 96
Watson, James, 26
Wayne Hills Baptist Church, 35
wedge strategy, 77
Weinberg, Steven, 186
well-tuned universe, 179
Wells, Jonathan, 74
West Virginia State University, 86
Whale, J. S., *Christian Doctrine*, 157
Whitcomb, John, *The Genesis Flood*, 32, 33
White, Bob, 165
Whittington, Harry, 168–169, 170
Willard, Dallas, 111
Williams, Charles, 174
Wise, Kurt, 11–29
   commitment to Christ, 12–13
   and creation science, 14
   curriculum based on attributes of God, 26
   as evangelist in college, 15
   Faith, Form, and Time, 22–23
   at Harvard, 17, 19–20
   impact of fire at Bryan, 24
   job loss, 25

   need for synthetic theory for biology and geology, 21
   suicide consideration, 12
   at University of Chicago, 14–15
   Wood and, 38
Wiseman, Donald, 159
Wittgenstein, Ludwig, 185
Wonderful Life (Gould), 167–168, 172
Wood, Todd, 21, 24, 31–45, 59
   background, 31
   at Bryan University, 41–45
   death of grandfather, 32
   doctoral dissertation, 40
   first meeting with grad students, 39
   Understanding the Pattern of Life, 40
YAC (yeast artificial chromosome), 35
young earth creationists, 7, 57, 205–207
   in Britain, 165
   dinosaurs and, 48
   Falk and, 127–128
   greatest problem, 203
   image for life, 58–59
   vs. Intelligent Design movement, 77
   Rana and, 91–92
   strength, 202–203
young earth, history of, 22
Young Life, 106
Z-DNA, 66, 74, 80

231

About the Author

Tim Stafford is Senior Writer for *Christianity Today* and the author of more than thirty books including *The Student Bible* (with Philip Yancey). His most recent publications are *Miracles: A Journalist Looks at Modern-Day Experiences of God's Power,* and *Birmingham* (a novel). Tim and his wife, Popie, have three children and live in Santa Rosa, California